Timesaver

NEWSPAPER ARTICLES TO GET TEENAGERS TALKING

By Peter Dainty

SCHOLASTIC

CONTENTS

INTRODUCTION   4

LIFESTYLE

1. How often do you touch people?   8
   'What do Puerto Ricans do 180 times an hour?'

2. You are what you drink   10
   'What your choice of coffee says about you'

3. Things you love the most   12
   'A Valentine card for the dog ...'

4. Going bananas   14
   'Yes, we have bananas - 30,000 of them'

5. Too much TV?   16
   'How to ration the time your child watches TV'

6. Shopping with Big Brother   18
   'The shopper snapper'

7. The computer games addict   20
   'Gameboys and girls stay in to play'

8. Glasses for your dog   22
   'For the pet whose sight has gone to the dogs'

MORAL ISSUES

9. Helping the homeless   24
   'From a Consul house to an Estately home / The police have a duty to every householder'

10. Compensation culture   28
    'Safeway leaflet crippled my dog / Writs a mad, mad world!'

11. Free money   32
    'Villagers strike it rich as they discover cash machine is doubling their money'

12. Starting again   34
    'The man who swapped lives'

13. Money matters   36
    'Pizza man gives away his millions / Lonely Beckham runs up a £433,000 hotel bill'

14. Charities   40
    'RNIB: Helping you live with sight loss'

15. Disciplining children   42
    'Should smacking ban get backing?'

WORK AND EDUCATION

16	International companies 'Hangin' on the Delhi Phone / Ain't life brand'	44
17	From teacher to plumber 'Biologist abandons vital research to double his salary fitting boilers / Skint boffin quits to be rich plumber'	48
18	Does punctuation matter? 'Never mind the punctuation, look at our low price's'	52
19	Does prison work? 'Italian crooks are helping with Inquiries'	54
20	The island doctor 'A new life on Jura is just what the doctor ordered'	56
21	A man's job? 'Gondoliers sink hopes of first woman driver'	58
22	The school day 'Lessons leave no time for play in Seoul'	60
23	Bullies at school '12 ways to beat bullies'	62

FOOD AND HEALTH

24	New foods 'Sweet strawmato is pick of the crop'	64
25	Too old to have children? 'Older Mom not so bad'	66
26	How deep can you go? 'The human submarine'	68
27	Better school meals 'iPod lure to cut down junk food'	70
28	The 12-year-old alcoholic 'Binge drinker aged 12'	72

WORLD ISSUES

29	Opportunities for wealth 'Chocolate isles struggle to avert the 'curse' of oil/ What a difference a day makes'	74
30	The old soldiers 'Alan Hamilton joins veterans of the South Lancashire Regiment on their return to Normandy'	78
31	Global warming 'In the land where life is on hold'	80
32	Chemical alert 'The 75 toxic chemicals in our blood'	82

ANSWER KEYS 84

INTRODUCTION

For a language teacher, there are few things more exciting than a classroom discussion that really works, especially if your students get the chance to practise the vocabulary they have just learned. Everyone can make a positive and equal contribution to the debate. Unfortunately, good classroom discussions like this are notoriously difficult to organise. Teachers usually give the following three main reasons for this:
1 My students weren't very interested in the topic.
2 The class didn't know enough of the key vocabulary.
3 I found it difficult to involve everyone in the discussion. There were two or three people who talked a lot, but the others didn't contribute enough.

This book has been specially designed to help you overcome these three problems and to give you a format for discussions that can really work.

The structure of the book

Each unit begins with an authentic article, most with a strong 'human interest' element. Many classes find it easier to get involved in a topic if the starting point is a real life, human drama rather than a list of facts and figures.

The articles have been chosen to help 'personalise' the topic and make students feel the debate is about real life situations rather than something abstract, academic and theoretical. So, for example, the issue of global warming is approached through the eyes of a Zambian farmer called Julius Njame whose crops have been ruined by weeks of drought. Similarly, the starting point for a discussion on homelessness is the real life experience of a woman called Ann Naysmith who, after a career as a pianist, fell on hard times and ended up living in a battered Ford car on a street in west London.

A small clock icon at the top of each unit gives the approximate time needed to complete the tasks. Most can be completed in a 40-minute lesson, though some will require 50 minutes or longer.

Getting started

Each unit has the headline that accompanied the article when it was originally published, along with a relevant photograph. You may like to use these to get students to predict what the article might be about before you go on to read the text. For example, read the headline and ask the following questions.

Gondoliers sink hopes of first woman driver

Where was the photograph taken? Have you ever seen a woman doing this kind of job before? Why is the collocation 'sink the hopes of' particularly suitable for a story about gondoliers?

Approaching the text

The second problem mentioned above is identifying and then teaching the language items your class will need to discuss an issue fluently.

How you use the blackboard can be crucial in getting a discussion to work. Write up key language items from the article (these are usually highlighted in the vocabulary and comprehension exercises that follow). You can then go through (and if necessary add to) this list before starting the discussion.

Keep these useful words and phrases on the board during the discussion. This will give students a point of reference as they try to collect their thoughts and express their opinions. Students are more likely to try out a new verb that you have just taught them if they can look up at the board and check which preposition it goes with.

You can also revise these language items after the discussion and highlight those words and phrases that are particularly worth learning.

Being able to see 20 or 30 key language items before, during and after a conversation can make many students feel a lot more confident.

Getting everyone involved

How can you make sure everyone contributes to a discussion? If you find that only a few people are taking part in the conversation, switch tack and encourage students to talk directly about their own experiences rather than asking them a question that needs some detailed knowledge of the subject.

For example, in the article about the diver Tanya Streeter who can go 120 metres underwater on a single breath of air, you would need some background information to answer a question such as *What happens to your body when you go this deep under the ocean?* However, at the end of the text, Tanya says she would be terrified to go up Mount Everest. So if you ask a question such as *What is the scariest thing you have ever done?*, you know that everyone in the group can give you an answer and, crucially, each of those answers is equally valid.

If you develop the discussion in this way, there are no right or wrong answers. This can make some classes more forthcoming.

However, get to know what your class like best and adjust the lesson accordingly. Some groups love the cut and thrust of debate, marshalling facts and figures to prove a case. Others do not want to be confrontational and prefer a discussion in which everyone has their own point of view or anecdote to tell.

The follow-up exercises

If you have time left at the end of the discussion, there is also a follow-up exercise involving group writing or role play. Everyone can be involved, using the language they have met in the article or articles in a realistic or personalised context.

Project work

The units in this book are designed as one-off classroom exercises, but you can also use them as source material for a more general project on newspapers and the press.

For example, get students to find the differences between the language, style, presentation, format, typeface, vocabulary, content and use of photographs in the different types of papers.

If you want to give your students a brief introduction to the press in the UK, you may find the comprehension and discussion exercises on the next two pages a good place to begin.

The next pages also include the newspaper websites, which are often updated very early in the morning, so you can read some of the articles online before the actual papers have hit the newsstands.

NEWSPAPER ARTICLES TO GET TEENAGERS TALKING

British newspapers

You can divide British newspapers into three broad categories: the popular 'red tops', (*The Sun, The Mirror, The News of the World* etc.), the 'middle market' press such as *The Daily Mail* and *The Daily Express*, and the so-called 'serious papers' (*The Times, The Independent, The Guardian* etc.).

RED TOPS
'Red tops' are called this because they all have a red logo. The content is mostly gossip, sensational news and controversy with lots of stories about celebrities such as David Beckham and his wife, Victoria. They are all tabloid, the smallest size of paper (approximately 29cm by 35cm).

MIDDLE MARKET
The 'middle market' papers are also tabloid and cover more serious issues as well as gossip and controversy.

SERIOUS
The 'serious' papers have traditionally been broadsheet, the largest size of newspaper (approximately 34cm by 58cm), although now many of them are tabloid or other sizes.

Many of the daily papers have sister papers, which are separate papers published by the same company on different days, usually on a Sunday.

Use the information on page 7 to complete Exercise 1.

Which paper (or papers) ...

a   has the biggest circulation? _____ The News of the World _____

b   has the smallest circulation? _____

c   is over 200 years old? _____

d   is only published on a Sunday? _____

e   sells more copies on Sunday than during the week? _____

f   is the most popular daily 'red-top'? _____

g   is the most popular 'middle market' paper? _____

h   is the most popular 'serious' paper? _____

i   is the sister paper of *The Sun*? _____

j   is published as a broadsheet? _____

Now discuss the following.

a   What are the equivalent 'red top', 'middle market' and 'serious' papers in your country? What sort of information do they contain?
b   What is your favourite paper? Why do you read it?
c   What makes a good newspaper?
d   Why do you think 'red tops' sell more copies than 'serious' papers?
e   Are you influenced by the newspapers that you read? Do they change the way you think about the world?
f   In the future, will people stop reading newspapers and get all their information from the internet or TV?

THE 'RED TOPS'

The Daily Mirror/Sunday Mirror
established: 1903
published: seven days a week
circulation: 1,670,000 during the week; 1,400,000 on Sundays
format: tabloid
website: www.mirror.co.uk

The Sun
established: 1964
published: Monday to Saturday
circulation: 3,190,000
format: tabloid
website: www.thesun.co.uk

The News of the World (sister paper to The Sun)
established: 1843
published: once a week, on Sundays
circulation: 3,730,000
format: tabloid
website: www.newsoftheworld.co.uk

The Daily Star/Star on Sunday
established: 1978
published: seven days a week
circulation: 795,000 during the week; 395,000 on Sundays
format: tabloid
website: www.dailystar.co.uk

The People
established: 1881
published: once a week; on Sundays
circulation: 870,000
format: tabloid
website: www.people.co.uk

THE 'MIDDLE MARKET'

The Daily Mail/Mail on Sunday
established: 1896
published: seven days a week
circulation: 2,340,000 (the same for the Sunday edition)
format: tabloid
website: www.dailymail.co.uk

The Daily Express/Sunday Express
established: 1900
published: seven days a week
circulation: 796,000 during the week; 871,000 on Sundays
format: tabloid
website: www.express.co.uk

THE 'SERIOUS' PAPERS

The Times/Sunday Times
established: 1785
published: seven days a week
circulation: 690,000 during the week; 1,390,000 on Sundays
format: tabloid during the week, broadsheet on Sundays
website: www.timesonline.co.uk

The Guardian
established: 1821
published: Monday to Saturday
circulation: 400,000
format: slightly bigger than a tabloid
website: www.guardian.co.uk

The Observer (the world's first Sunday paper and sister paper to The Guardian)
established: 1791
published: Sundays
circulation: 436,000
format: slightly bigger than a tabloid
website: www.observer.co.uk

The Telegraph/Sunday Telegraph
established: 1855
published: seven days a week
circulation: 903,000 during the week; 714,000 on Sundays
format: broadsheet
website: www.telegraph.co.uk

The Independent/Sunday Independent
established: 1986
published: seven days a week
circulation: 263,000 during the week; 225,000 on Sundays
format: tabloid
website: www.independent.co.uk

Lifestyle

1 How often do you touch people?

The American psychologist, Dr Sidney Jourard, has a fascinating job. He travels the world watching how people in different countries behave. He recently visited Puerto Rico, France and Britain to see how people greet and talk to each other. This article describes some of the things he found out.

1 Before you read, discuss the following.

How do you greet people in your country? Do you shake hands, bow or kiss each other on the cheek? How do you learn the right thing to do?

Do you greet friends and family differently from people you do not know?

Glossary

1 touchy: very sensitive
2 when it comes to: on the subject of
3 carried out: did
4 missing out: losing an opportunity
5 pumping: shaking very strongly, up and down
6 give off: transmit

WHAT PUERTO RICANS DO 180 TIMES AN HOUR, THE FRENCH 110 TIMES AN HOUR AND THE BRITISH NOT AT ALL

Britons are touchy when it comes to touching each other, according to a top psychologist.

He spent an hour in a coffee shop to count the number of times he saw one person touch another. *Not one did.*

But when he carried out the same survey in Puerto Rico, 180 people touched others. And in France there were 110 touches.

The psychologist, American Dr Sidney Jourard, recorded just two touches an hour in the United States.

It seems that most Britons and Americans are missing out. For surveys show that people like being touched.

Marriage counsellors have found that the happiest couples touch each other often.

Waitresses who touch their customers get larger tips than those who don't.

And nearly all doctors believe touch helps relieve patients' fear of treatment.

Routine

Research has also revealed, though, that there are times when a touch is not welcome.

Like a pumping handshake from someone we don't know well.

Or the hugging and kissing that is just a routine every time friends meet.

A young married woman admitted avoiding acquaintances who gave ritual hugs.

"It is too casual, and that irritates me," she said.

"I prefer touching to occur spontaneously, when I am engaged in a significant conversation with someone.

"In this atmosphere I have never withdrawn or feel the other individual withdraw from a touch."

People who don't want to be touched give off clues, say experts.

They may stiffen or back away. Eyes narrow and lips tighten.

But even if we don't like being touched, experts say a smile can make us feel better.

Smiling, which involves our 80 facial muscles, increases blood flow and triggers the production of "happy" brain chemicals.

But a frown restricts the blood supply, and that can leave us feeling low or depressed.

So let's have a big smile from you. And don't forget to keep in touch.

© Daily Mirror

2 As you read, complete the crossword with words from the text.

Across
4 causes, makes happen, provokes
5 a smile increases blood ...
6 to become tight
8 to become stiff
9 ordinary, everyday
10 to do naturally, unplanned, without thinking
11 people that you know but do not know very well

Down
1 annoys, makes angry
2 a confused, angry or unhappy look; the opposite of smile
3 signals, signs; they help you fill in a crossword
6 very sensitive
7 some people do not like a pumping ...

3 Choose the best answer.

a Dr Jourard ...
   (1) spent three hours in each coffee shop.
   (2) recorded 110 touches in Puerto Rico.
   (3) saw more touches in the US than in Britain.
b A touch ...
   (1) can help waitresses get bigger tips.
   (2) makes patients more afraid of treatment.
   (3) is always welcome.
c People ...
   (1) enjoy a pumping handshake from an acquaintance.
   (2) like routine, ritual hugs.
   (3) give off signals when they do not want to be touched.
d When you smile, ...
   (1) you get a pain in your jaw.
   (2) it reduces the blood flow in your face.
   (3) it makes you feel better.
e When you frown ...
   (1) you feel better.
   (2) it restricts the blood supply.
   (3) it triggers the production of happy chemicals.

4 Now discuss the following.

a Which of the following people is it appropriate to touch?

| your best friend | a teacher | a shop assistant |
| another student | a waitress | your friend's parents |

b When is it right or wrong to sit close to another person? Give some examples.
c When should you use a person's first name, surname or title? Do you use language differently with different kinds of people?
d Should you look at someone when you are talking to them?
e What can you learn about a person from their body language?
f Should you take your shoes off at the door when you visit someone's home? Should you eat all the food you are given when you visit someone? Are there any other social rules you can think of?
g Are these social rules important? Why/Why not? Do politeness and good manners really matter?
h Where do we learn these social rules? Is it from our families, school or from TV?
i Are these rules permanent or do they change from one generation to the next? What different social rules did your parents have?

5 Your town is about to host a major international conference and the organisers have asked you to provide delegates with a list of 'dos and don'ts' about what is considered polite and impolite in your area.

a In groups, write a brief guide to etiquette and social rules entitled 'Greeting, Meeting and Eating in this part of the world'. Use the language below.

*When you greet someone in this part of the world, you should _____, but never _____.
During a conversation, you should _____
but don't _____ as this is considered rude.
Use words like _____ and _____
These are all very polite.
As far as eating is concerned, always _____ or
_____ but never _____
At the end of a meal, don't _____
There are some subjects that you should avoid, such as _____, but feel free to talk about
_____ or _____
But please don't _____ or _____
as all these are considered inappropriate.
We'd also recommend you to _____
We hope you enjoy your stay with us and that you'll come back soon.*

b Then present your suggestions to the rest of the class.

NEWSPAPER ARTICLES TO GET TEENAGERS TALKING Lifestyle

2 You are what you drink

This article appeared in the *Lifestyle* section of *The Daily Express* and it suggests that you can tell a lot about a person from the kind of coffee they drink.

1) Before you read, discuss the following.
Do you think a person's preferred drink can tell you anything about their personality?
Ask three people in your class which of the following types of coffee they prefer.

| espresso | latte | decaffeinated | cafetiere | cappuccino |
| black | iced | instant | filter | none of them |

Do you think differently about anyone now you know what type of coffee they like?

Glossary

1 a shot of: a small amount of
2 wimpish: weak and frightened
3 speak their mind: say what they think
4 decaf: short for decaffeinated
5 dip your toe in the water: cautiously try a new thing
6 take the plunge: make a commitment
7 shies away from: avoids
8 the cutting edge: the latest, most modern (fashion, technology etc)
9 no-nonsense: practical, functional, business-like
10 flighty: unreliable
11 no-frills: no-nonsense, practical, functional
12 to click (with someone): to like (someone) from the first moment

2) As you read, match the words from the article 1–9 with their meanings a–i.

1 workwise   a) improve
2 homely   b) attitude, philosophy
3 aspirational   c) extrovert, full of life
4 etiquette   d) determined, focused
5 enhance   e) prefer, like
6 outlook   f) as far as work is concerned
7 bubbly   g) ambitious
8 favour   h) home-loving
9 single-minded   i) politeness, correct behaviour

3) Which coffee drinker ...

1 has a bubbly personality? _cappuccino_
2 is frightened of commitment but believes in true love? _____
3 doesn't care what others think? _____
4 is practical, honest, open and loyal? _____
5 is a home-loving person who speaks their mind? _____
6 is easily bored? _____
7 is unreliable and always on the move? _____
8 hates confrontation and goes with the flow? _____
9 likes time to think things through? _____
10 believes in politeness and social rules? _____
11 puts their career ahead of home life and may seem a little dull? _____
12 has a balanced approach to life? _____

4) Now discuss the following.

1 How true is this survey for you and your class?
2 Do you usually read surveys like this? Are they revealing or rubbish?
3 Do you believe in horoscopes? Is a *Gemini* (born between 21 May and 20 June) really different from a *Capricorn* (22 December–19 January)?
4 Chinese Astrology suggests that your character comes from the year of your birth. For example, a *Goat* (born in 1979 or 1991) is friendly but easily led, a *Monkey* (1980 or 1992) is intelligent but untidy and a *Buffalo* (1985 or 1997) is reliable but stubborn. Is this true?

5) A newspaper has asked you to do a similar article based on one of the themes below. In groups, choose one of the themes and then come up with five different categories (for example, *music* might include *rock and roll, hip hop, folk, classical* and *jazz*).

| clothes | food | music | hobbies | films | sport |

a Write sentences for each category. Use language from the article and the following.

People who like ... are ... and ...
They often ... but never ...

b Now try your survey with the other groups. Ask them which of your five categories they like best. Then explain what their choices mean.

What your choice of coffee says about you

Are you a frappuccino poser or an espresso loner? TV's body language expert Judi James tells JAMES MOORE how the coffee you drink reveals more than you think

ESPRESSO
The drink: A strong coffee made by forcing hot water through crushed coffee beans.
Judi's verdict: It's a drink that's over quickly, so the drinker isn't necessarily a very sociable person or, at least, tends to get bored easily and moves on quickly from situations. Espresso drinkers can be loners and certainly have attitudes – they might be sarcastic and aggressive if pushed. When it comes to relationships, they're tough and know exactly what they want. Workwise, they're always trying to achieve something they can't quite reach.

LATTE
The drink: A shot of espresso with plenty of milk, often served in a glass.
Judi's verdict: A nice, cosy type of person who doesn't like risk or danger. A homely sort who is likely to be loyal to their family or partner. An ideal date for a Latte drinker would probably be a night in on the sofa with a movie – and a latte! They like comfortable surroundings and long chats with good friends. Anyone who orders a decaf latte is worryingly wimpish, but probably an individual who will openly speak their mind. The question is, would anyone be listening?

DECAF
The drink: Coffee – without the caffeine.
Judi's verdict: A worrier – not just about their health. Decaf drinkers feel scared by a lot of things in life and though they will dip their toes into the water when it comes to new experiences, they rarely take the plunge long-term. This person likes to go with the flow, to follow the crowd, but shies away from confrontation. When it comes to relationships they are often commitment-phobes although they do need other people and are always searching for the perfect relationship.

CAFETIERE
The drink: Served in a glass container with a plunger for filtering out the solids.
Judi's verdict: It's all to do with the gadget rather than the coffee. This is a person obsessed with appearances. They're also someone who likes to see themselves on the way up – an aspirational person, but one who likes etiquette and rules. The cafetiere drinker likes to be thought of as stylish and a bit continental. When it comes to relationships, they will choose a partner to enhance their status.

CAPPUCCINO
The drink: Made with heated milk with froth on the top and often a sprinkling of chocolate.
Judi's verdict: A lively extrovert with an optimistic outlook on life. Like the coffee they are bubbly but not shallow. Cappuccino drinkers aren't unduly worried about being at the cutting edge of fashion but they do like having nice objects and attractive people around them. They are sexy and tactile – especially if they're the type to sprinkle their own chocolate on top. They have a balanced approach to life.

BLACK COFFEE
The drink: A large cup of coffee – taken without milk.
Judi's verdict: This is a no-nonsense drink that reflects the people who drink it. Black coffee drinkers are likely to be practical, decisive and business-like. Some people might find them a little dull, but, in fact they are individuals with some sophistication and probably focused on their career rather than leisure and home life. In relationships this is a person who is confident and happy to take the lead.

FRAPPUCCINO
The drink: Any variation on iced coffee.
Judi's verdict: A bit of a poser. They like to stay at the cutting edge of the coffee market as in the rest of life. When new trends appear they are likely to follow and see themselves as trend-setters. There's a chance people will see them as a bit style over substance. At home they favour modern décor over antiques. They're also a bit flighty – friendships and relationships tend to come and go. Frappuccino drinkers are social butterflies who shy away from long-term relationships – they want to keep moving.

INSTANT
The drink: Just add water and/or milk to the granules.
Judi's verdict: This is a no-frills type of person, somebody who takes life as it comes or wants to appear that way. They like a laugh. They tend to get a lift easily and are honest and open. Instant drinkers like the simple pleasures of life, like going to the pub, but they aren't that adventurous in their career. In relationships they are likely to be loyal but may not provide a huge amount of excitement.

FILTER
The drink: Made by slowly pouring hot water through crushed coffee beans in a coffee filter.
Judi's verdict: An individualist who doesn't worry about kudos or what others think. They are single-minded and know what they want from life. But they like time to think things over. They don't enjoy being put in high-pressure situations but are thorough in their work and will see a job through. Filter drinkers have a strong personality and as far as relationships go, if someone doesn't click straight away they aren't going to be bothered.

© Daily Express

3 Things you love the most

A Valentine card for the dog ...

... and the cat, Mum, Dad, Granny and Grandad. Proof that the special day for lovers has fallen victim to a cynical marketing machine

by **BEN SHEPPARD**

SO who says Valentine's Day has become a cynical marketing exercise rather than a celebration of true love?

Well, anyone who has been tempted to buy a card for their granny, brother or pet cat. Or their parents, sisters, sons, daughters, nieces and nephews.

More and more shops are getting in on the act by selling Valentine cards specifically *not* aimed at couples in love.

Poems inside the cards include lines such as 'Happy Val's Day to a son who stands out from the crowd. Now don't go all red but it must be said, you make everybody feel proud.'

Another reads: 'Wherever there's laughter and good times, kindness and gentleness too, there are two special people who make it all happen – a grandma and granddad like you.'

Yet another says: 'Daddy, you're so good to me, you're such a lot of fun. And of all the daddies in the world, you're just the nicest one.'

A message from the family dog reads: 'Happy Valentine's Day from the one who gives you unconditional puppy love.'

Clinton Cards, which sells many of the cards, would not comment on whether it was entering the true spirit of Valentine's Day.

But a spokesman said: 'These cards are increasingly popular and show that people want to express affection for the other loved ones in their lives as well as their partners. Romantic love is not the only kind.'

Some 32 million cards will be sent this year, of which 20 million will be delivered by hand.

The Royal Mail said the record levels are partly explained by the new fashion for sending cards to family and friends as well as lovers.

Valentine's Day is becoming more expensive each year, with £40 million being spent on flowers.

Relationship expert Jenni Trent Hughes warned people off 'platonic cards'. She said: 'They are an American idea that has come over here. A card could help a lonely grandparent, but most sons would not appreciate a card from their parents at all.

'I just can't understand cards to or from pets. One wife I know gets a card from her cat, but not one from her husband. That's a bad sign. I advise a simple gift between lovers.' About 23 million romantic text messages will be sent and if you receive a mystifying text that reads ILYMTTASITS, don't worry.

It's just that someone Loves You More Than There Are Stars In The Sky.

© The Mail on Sunday

NEWSPAPER ARTICLES TO GET TEENAGERS TALKING Lifestyle

Most people celebrate Valentine's Day (February 14th) by sending a romantic card to their boyfriend, girlfriend, husband or wife. But a company called Clinton Cards have now come up with a new idea. They make Valentine's cards for our grandparents, friends and even our pets with their own special messages.

1. Before you read, discuss the following.

What do you think of the idea of sending Valentine's cards to your family, friends and pets?
Would you send a card to your best friend or your cat?

Glossary

1. fallen victim to: become a victim of, suffered
2. getting in on the act: joining in, doing the same thing
3. puppy love: child-like love
4. some 32 million: approximately, about 32 million

2. As you read, answer the questions to find the meaning of these words.

a. If the marketing machine is *cynical*, is it selfish or unselfish?
b. Is your *niece* the daughter of your brother or sister, or the son of your brother or sister?
c. Is your *nephew* the daughter of your brother or sister, or the son of your brother or sister?
d. If you *stand out* from the crowd, are you hidden or visible?
e. If you *go red*, are you embarrassed or comfortable?
f. If your love is *unconditional*, is it selfish or unselfish?
g. Does *increasingly* mean more and more, or about the same?
h. Is *platonic* love based on friendship or romance?
i. If you *appreciate* a card, do you hate it or value it?
j. If the text is *mystifying*, is it easy to understand or difficult to understand?

3. Choose the best answer.

a. According to the article, platonic cards ...
   (1) are becoming more popular.
   (2) are becoming less popular.
   (3) are not sold in shops.
b. The article mentions ...
   (1) a card sent by a cousin.
   (2) a card sent by a dog.
   (3) a card sent by a teacher.
c. This year, ...
   (1) 32 million cards will be delivered by hand.
   (2) Valentine's Day will be cheaper than last year.
   (3) we will spend £40 million on flowers.

d. Jenni Trent Hughes says ...
   (1) platonic cards are a great idea.
   (2) a lonely grandparent would appreciate a card.
   (3) most sons would be happy to get a card from their parents.

4. Now discuss the following.

a. Do you send Valentine's cards? What about Father's Day cards or Mother's Day cards?
b. Do you have any special days in your country, e.g for teachers/grandparents/pets, or 'national day'? If so, describe what happens.
c. What is your favourite festival or annual celebration? What happens and why do you like it so much?
d. Are 'special days' like these just a way of making money, or are they important?

5. The United Nations have announced plans to introduce a new event called World Friendship Day, to be celebrated on June 8th every year. They have asked your group to come up with some suggestions. Consider these things.

a. What could happen on World Friendship Day? How would people celebrate? What would they do? Use some of the following ideas.

| parties | dinners | fireworks | carnival | street theatre |

b. Would there be special programmes on TV? Would everyone get a day off school?
c. Would there be an international event, such as a pop concert or sports event? If so, what would happen and who would be invited?
d. Make a typical World Friendship Day card with an illustration and message, or write a text message.

Present your messages and ideas to the rest of the class. Use the following language.

On World Friendship Day, we would like to see _____

The main event would be _____

People would send cards or text messages to _____

They would also celebrate the day by _____

The best part of World Friendship Day would be _____

It would be a great idea because _____

4 Going bananas

Yes, we have bananas – 30,000 of them.
Nelson surveys square's latest installation

By Arifa Akbar

WELL BEFORE dawn, the early birds around Trafalgar Square realised something was amiss. Bananas, hundreds of them, were being piled in a huge heap. That they were positioned next to the National Gallery offered a clue. The hundreds became 30,000 by 5am and London's most famous square had its latest art installation.

The bananas provoked much scratching of heads as the crowds of tourists and passers-by pondered what the latest statement on the North Terrace could possibly mean.

Its creator, Doug Fishbone, was giving away few clues. He and 20 dedicated friends had arrived in a truck at 1.30am yesterday with six tons of Cavendish bananas to create the eight-foot-high mound. This, though, was a temporary installation and by 3pm, Mr Fishbone, a 35-year-old New Yorker, had begun to dismantle his creation and distributed all the bananas to passers-by.

During the day, the artwork was described in a variety of ways: a post-modern work of staggering genius; a cunning marketing ploy; a chimpanzee's dream. But by the time the bananas were given away, no one seemed to care. A scrum of tourists, office workers and students battled to bag themselves a bunch. "I'm going to sell these at the Tube station. If he can call a bunch of bananas art, then I think I can too – and make a profit," said Aidan Ashton Griffiths, 16, from North London.

Two Russian women, who reckoned the artist's message was one of communist abundance ("to each according to his needs"), had arrived early with carrier bags to fill with free fruit. "We were told about this by the guide in our hotel. These will be our souvenirs," said Emilia Finkel, 70, from St Petersburg.

Art students guarded the work to ensure it was not dismantled prematurely by bystanders and many were admonished for attempting to eat the artwork.

Despite being pressured by the public for an explanation, Fishbone remained silent. So the crowd resorted to their own theories. Some thought it was a war memorial. An Australian couple thought it might be the work of activists protesting against banana importation and Marxists felt it was a comment on capitalist greed. Art students admired its vivid colour and composition.

Fishbone said the discussion was exactly what he had set out to achieve. "A lot of people have asked me what it means but I'm stepping back. I want this to involve the audience. It's such a big physical presence and changes so much in different contexts that I cannot honestly say any more whether it still has its original meaning," he said.

He said he was inspired to build the sculpture while living in South America and had created five similar installations in Ecuador, Costa Rica, Poland and New York. He explained: "I was living in Ecuador and I came across a heap of plantains dumped on the road to sell. I stopped in my tracks and thought that it looked magnificent and wanted to see it in an artistic context."

Critics were reluctant to accept the sculpture as anything other than a prosaic heap of bananas.

Anna Somers Cocks, founding editor of The Art Newspaper, said the "wow factor" had to be distinguished from its actual meaning, if any, while Brian Sewell condemned it as a hollow "attention grabbing" exercise. "It is merely the Elephant Man syndrome when people congregate to see something freakish," he said. "I could grab the same kind of public attention by standing on my head. What is not art … is a heap of bananas in Trafalgar Square."

And what about dissent from the crowd of passers-by? John and Sonia Kemp, both 70, from Walton Creek, near San Francisco, were mystified: "When the folks back home see these pictures, they are going to think the Brits are a bunch of loonies," said Mr Kemp.

© The Independent

NEWSPAPER ARTICLES TO GET TEENAGERS TALKING — Lifestyle

Doug Fishbone is an artist who creates installations, in which everyday objects are put together in unusual situations. For one of these installations, he built a huge pile of bananas outside the National Gallery in London. Later that afternoon, Fishbone dismantled his art and gave all the bananas away.

1 Before you read, discuss the following.

What do you think tourists, passers-by and art critics made of Doug Fishbone's pile of bananas?
How would you react?

Glossary

1 going bananas: going mad
2 Nelson = Lord Nelson, the Admiral who fought Napoleon Bonaparte at the Battle of Trafalgar. Nelson's statue stands in Trafalgar Square.
3 scratching of heads: confusion, puzzlement
4 to bag: to get (something in demand)
5 the Tube: the London Underground network
6 plantain: a tropical fruit similar to a banana
7 Elephant Man: a Victorian man who attracted attention because of his unusual looks
8 loonies: mad people

2 As you read, match the words from the article 1–9 with their meaning a–i.

1 passers-by   a) take down (the opposite of build)
2 pondered   b) large quantities of
3 dismantle   c) criticised, told off
4 abundance   d) found or met (by chance)
5 prematurely   e) people going past
6 admonished   f) thought about
7 came across   g) weird, strange, unnatural
8 freakish   h) very puzzled
9 mystified   i) too early

3 Now circle T (True) or F (False).

a Trucks started bringing the bananas before 5am. T / F
b Doug Fishbone was happy to talk about his installation. T / F
c The installation was built to last. T / F
d The installation was dismantled just before midnight. T / F
e A respectful queue formed as the installation was taken down. T / F
f Mrs Finkel brought a suitcase to fill with bananas. T / F
g Doug Fishbone has created similar installations before. T / F
h He was inspired by a pile of plantains in a supermarket. T / F
i Art critic Brian Sewell loved the work. T / F
j The Kemps, an American couple, did not understand the installation. T / F

4 Now discuss the following.

a What do you think of Doug Fishbone's installation? Is it a work of art or a waste of time and money?
b What is art? Is it important? Why/Why not?
c Is there a difference between high art (opera, ballet) and popular art (soap operas, pop music)? Which is more important?
d Is a fresco by Leonardo da Vinci any better than graffiti art spray-painted on a wall?
e Should governments subsidise the arts? If you answer yes, which of the following kinds of art would you give funding to?

| installations | folk music | pop music |
| opera | theatre | buskers | poetry |

f Would money be better spent on something more useful, like medical research?

Fact file

Go to www.christojeanneclaude.net to see the work of the world's most famous installation artists, Christo and his wife Jeanne-Claude. Their work includes:
• stretching a 12,780 square metre orange curtain across the Rifle Valley in California.
• wrapping the German Parliament building in 75,000 metres of silver fabric and 8,000 metres of rope.
• an installation of 1,340 blue umbrellas (each six metres tall) in Ibaraki, Japan.

5 Your group have been asked to make a piece of installation art for a modern art exhibition. Read the Fact file. Then, using the objects in the room around you, create your own installation.

a Decide what objects you are going to use.
b Give your installation a name.
c Build it. Write a short text explaining what the piece means.
d Show and explain your installation to the rest of the class. Use the following language.

Our installation is called ... and it consists of ...
We gave it this name because ...
The meaning of this piece is ...

Ask other groups what they think of it.

5 Too much TV?

How to ration the time your child watches TV

FROM BEN MACINTYRE IN NEW YORK

Parents too weak-willed, indulgent or exhausted to insist that their children turn off the television can take hope from a new gadget introduced in the United States. TV Allowance is an electronic disciplinarian that permits each member of the family a specific amount of viewing time and turns off the set when it runs out.

The machine was invented by an amateur scientist from Florida who said that his family life was being destroyed by battles with his children over the amount of time they spent in front of the box. It went on sale in America last month for $99 (£55). It is being adapted to European sets and is expected to reach Britain early next year.

The principle is simple: every member of the family is allotted an individual code which must be punched into the machine to turn the television on; each minute watched deducts a minute from that person's viewing allocation. The inventor, Randal Levenson, said that the machine teaches the young self-discipline and discrimination and, moreover, instils the essentials of capitalism since children can save their viewing time, barter it with each other or team up to maximise their resources.

"Initially I invented it just so I could stop yelling at my kids over the television, but it's really more of a teaching tool than an authoritarian device," Mr Levenson said.

"It teaches kids budgeting techniques, the art of the deal and business ethics."

Parents can programme the machine not to turn on at certain times (mealtimes, or during homework hours) and, like most parental

restrictions, it is unfair: parents are able to allocate themselves unlimited viewing time.

A recent survey revealed that the average American teenager spends three hours a day in front of the television, but authorities on child care are divided over whether a machine such as TV Allowance is the way to reduce television time, let alone maintain harmonious family relations. Some child psychologists argue that children should be weaned off television by persuasion and consultation and that house rules should be enforced by parents, not gadgets.

A number of satisfied customers report that the new contraption has successfully persuaded their children to look for other forms of entertainment. Others have found that their children simply alter their viewing habits: turning off the television during commercials, forcing younger siblings to surrender their viewing codes and refusing to watch anything recommended by their parents unless it is taken off the parents' viewing time.

© The Times

NEWSPAPER ARTICLES TO GET TEENAGERS TALKING — Lifestyle

A recent survey shows that British children aged 11-16 watch an average of 26 hours of television a week. This article is about a new machine that can be programmed to decide how much TV we all watch.

1 Before you read, discuss the following.

How much television do you watch a day?
Is watching television for 26 hours a week too much, too little or just about right?
Do you think the number of hours we watch should be restricted?

Glossary

1 the box: television
2 punched into: typed in
3 discrimination: knowing what is good and bad (in this text; a more common use means *prejudice*)
4 authorities: experts
5 be weaned off something: be helped get over an addiction to or need for something

2 As you read, answer the questions to find the meaning of these words.

a Does *ration* mean limit or increase?
b Does *indulgent* mean too cruel or too kind?
c Does *runs out* mean starts or finishes?
d Does *punched into* mean using your fist or using your finger?
e Does *deducts* mean adds or takes away?
f Does *instils* mean teaches or makes you afraid of?
g Does *barter* mean exchange or add?
h Does *team up* mean work together or fight with each other?
i Does *yelling* mean whispering or shouting?
j Does *siblings* mean brothers and sisters or your best friends?

3 Now circle T (True) or F (False).

a When your viewing time is finished, TV Allowance turns off the TV. T / F
b The inventor, Randal Levenson, is a professional scientist. T / F
c Each member of the family has their own individual number to type in. T / F
d You can 'sell' your viewing time to other family members. T / F
e Mr Levenson used to shout at his children a lot. T / F
f You can programme the gadget to turn the TV off during mealtimes. T / F
g Parents must have the same viewing time as children. T / F
h American children watch television on average for five hours a day. T / F
i Most child care experts have doubts about the gadget. T / F
j Children learn how to exploit the gadget. T / F
k Some children turn off the TV when the adverts are on to save their time. T / F
l Some children only watch programmes their parents want them to watch. T / F

4 Now discuss the following.

a How important is television in your life? Could you live without it?
b Do you think TV Allowance is a good idea?
c How would you feel if you were restricted to an hour's TV a day? What sort of TV programme would you give up?
d Do you like TV adverts? Are you influenced by the adverts you see on TV?
e Is there too much violence and bad language on TV?
f How has television changed the world in the last 50 years?
g Do you think people will watch more or less TV in the future?

5 A new satellite channel is about to start broadcasting in your area. They have asked you to come up with ideas for new programmes for teenagers aged 16 to 19. With your group, plan a schedule of programmes for Saturday from 6pm to midnight.

a Give the satellite channel a name.
b Decide how many different shows you want to have (soap operas, documentaries, music programmes, films etc.).
c Decide how long each programme should be.
d Present your ideas to the class.

Have a class vote to decide on the best programmes. How many of you would watch this kind of channel?

6 Shopping with Big Brother

The shopper snapper

Caught on camera as you pick up a product

By **Sean Poulter**
Consumer Affairs Correspondent

TESCO is testing a 'Big Brother' anti-theft system in which high-value items picked up off the shelf automatically trigger cameras to take a picture of the shopper.

A microchip the size of a grain of sand is attached to the product and communicates via radio waves with a reading device behind the shelf.

When the product is picked up, the radio connection is broken and this causes the camera to take a photograph.

This image is destroyed if the product is paid for through the till. Otherwise it can be retained to identify and prosecute a thief.

The trial, masterminded by Cambridge University's Auto-ID Centre, has been operating at a Tesco store in the city.

The product used was Gillette Mach 3 razor refills, which are shoplifted more often and in greater quantity than any other products in Britain and Europe.

They cost up to £6.97 each, yet because the packs are relatively small they can be easily concealed.

Marks & Spencer, Woolworths and Asda are already planning to introduce the computer chips, while many others are expected to follow suit.

However, civil liberty groups have protested about the scheme, saying it is an infringement of privacy.

And some opponents complain that the chips could be embedded in clothes, allowing stores to track people as they move about stores or the high street.

The technology has already evoked a backlash in the U.S. Benetton dropped plans to use the chips in pullovers following a threatened international boycott. Outside the Tesco trial store, protestor Damien Lawson was handing out leaflets yesterday. He said: 'If this trial is successful, a broader range of goods will be tagged.

'Tags could be buried in clothes and other items and you could be bristling with these chips. You would be transmitting without your knowledge personal information about where you shop and what you buy and how you pay that could be retrieved by anyone with the proper equipment.'

Professor Joshua Bamfield, of Nottingham's Centre for Retail Research, said he believed most families would be relaxed about the technology particularly since the cost to retailers and honest consumers of shoplifting is £800 million a year.

'People can be reassured that these pictures will be eliminated from the system in a matter of hours.

'All our research shows that people have confidence in CCTV. It reduces crime and fear of crime.

'I don't think ordinary shoppers would be anxious. If people were really worried about others knowing their shopping habits they would not have a loyalty card.'

The professor said the technology had many potential benefits. The tiny chips could be put on household computers and family treasures to help return stolen goods to their owner.

The chips are sophisticated enough to hold information on the name and address of the genuine owner.

Tesco insisted that its main interest in the system was 'to ensure our shelves are full and free up staff to help shoppers.'

A spokesman added: 'There were clear signs in the store about the use of the CCTV cameras, so customers knew what was going on. We would never compromise the privacy of our customers.'

THE TOP TEN GOODS STOLEN FROM SHOPS

1. Razors and razor blades
2. DVD movie blockbusters
3. Alcohol – particularly whisky, gin and alcopops
4. Women's clothing
5. Cosmetics – particularly lipsticks and compacts
6. Toiletries and aftershave
7. Perfume and fragrances
8. Lingerie
9. Computer games
10. Menswear/boyswear – including football strips

© Daily Mail

Lifestyle

In his book *1984*, the writer George Orwell describes a world in which the government (known as Big Brother) watches and films people all the time. Nobody is free and Big Brother knows everything about everyone. This article describes how shops and supermarkets are now using extraordinary Big Brother technology in an attempt to stop shoplifting.

① Before you read, discuss the following.

Have you seen CCTV (closed circuit television) cameras in shopping centres that film you as you shop?
Do they bother you? Or do they make you feel safer and more comfortable?

Glossary

1 snapper: something that takes snaps (photos)
2 Tesco, Marks and Spencer, Woolworths, Asda: major supermarket chains
3 masterminded: organised
4 ID: identification
5 Gillette Mach 3: a brand of disposable razor
6 tagged: fitted with a microchip 'tag'
7 bristling with: full of
8 a loyalty card: a store card giving discounts to loyal customers

② As you read, answer the questions to find the meaning of these words.

a If you *trigger* a reaction, do you start it or stop it?
b Does *attached* mean connected to or far away from?
c If you *prosecute* someone, do you let them off or take them to court?
d If you *follow suit*, do you copy someone else or act differently?
e If something is *embedded*, is it on the surface or inside?
f Does to *track* mean to follow or to be followed?
g If there is a *backlash*, do people react positively or negatively?
h Is a *pullover* something you wear or something you eat?
i If you *retrieve* information, do you send it or collect it?
j Does *sophisticated* mean primitive or advanced?

③ Now choose the best answer.

a Tesco are putting microchips ...
 (1) in some of their cheapest products.
 (2) in a few of their most expensive products.
 (3) in all of their products in all of their stores.
b When you pick up the Gillette Mach 3 razor refills, ...
 (1) a hidden camera takes a photograph of you.
 (2) a light flashes at the till.
 (3) a security guard will start watching you.
c According to Tesco, ...
 (1) the photograph is destroyed when you buy the product.
 (2) they would not use the photograph in court.
 (3) Gillette Mach 3 refills are difficult to steal.
d Civil liberty groups ...
 (1) are in favour of the new system.
 (2) will wait and see how the trials go.
 (3) are opposed to the scheme, saying it infringes privacy.
e Professor Bamfield suggests that ...
 (1) the public hate the idea of tagging products.
 (2) microchip technology will reduce shoplifting.
 (3) CCTV increases crime.
f The things shoplifters like to take most are ...
 (1) used for shaving.
 (2) used to smell nice.
 (3) used to wear.

④ Discuss the following.

a How do you feel about supermarkets taking photographs in this way? Is it 'an infringement of your privacy' or a sensible way of preventing shoplifting?
b Scientists say that the technology Tesco is using could easily be applied to people. For example, if a child were tagged, parents would know where they were 24 hours a day. Would this be a good idea?
c Do you care if people collect information about you?
d Would you be happy with ...
 • a doctor keeping your medical records?
 • a college having details of all your exam results?
 • a bank knowing how you spend your money?
 • the police having a sample of your DNA?
 • the government knowing your political opinions?
 • an identity card that carries your fingerprints?
 • satellites watching you from space?

⑤ The Ministry of Education wants to put ten CCTV cameras in your school. Divide into two groups, one representing the Ministry, the other representing the students and staff of your school.

Group 1: The Ministry group should discuss two things: where to put these ten cameras and how to explain the benefits of CCTV to the students and the staff.
Group 2: The School group should come up with arguments against the cameras, saying why you do not want Big Brother at your school.

a Group 1 present your arguments to the other group.
b Group 2 present your views to the Ministry.
c Take a class vote about whether to have the cameras or not.

NEWSPAPER ARTICLES TO GET TEENAGERS TALKING   Lifestyle

7 The computer games addict

This article is about a 13-year-old boy who is addicted to computer games. He loves them so much that his mother says they have become a kind of drug for him and the only time he seems really happy is when he is on the computer, playing a game.

1 Before you read, discuss the following.
Do you ever play games on your computer? What are your favourites? What do you like about them? Could you live without them? Do you think they are good or bad?

Buy a computer, one mother explains, and life can never be the same again.

Gameboys and girls stay in to play

Carolyn Roden

Like many 13 year olds, my son is a computer games hermit, emerging only to be fed and watered. Recently, to reassure me that he was not addicted, he volunteered not to touch the computer for a week. I kept a close eye on him for signs of cold turkey but apart from the fact that he recorded the music of his favourite games, so that he could listen to them on his Walkman, there was not one.

On the other hand, both his sister and I suffered as his boredom increased: I had not realised how we have created a life without him. Suddenly he was under our feet, muttering obscenities and flicking TV channels in the middle of our favourite programmes.

What he seemed to have lost was the sense that there was anything worthwhile to do other than indulge in the challenge of computer games. Suggestions from me to go and read, swim or play badminton got a grunt and a dark look. I guess the adrenaline rush of moving up a level on Lemmings cannot be compared with a gentle read or a few lengths of the local pool.

It may take another 10 years or so before society really knows the mental and physical effects of computer games on the young. Until then, parents can only feel their way in the dark as to how much and how often the games are allowed to be played.

My son and I have compromised on two computer-free days a week, plus a half-day at weekends. But the two free days seem to have become moveable feasts – they were to be Mondays and Wednesdays but very often I will get a telephone call from him after school, asking to swap days as he has got hooked into a game at a friend's house.

However, even on computer-free days we have negotiated that he can use the computer for things that I consider creative or useful, such as chess or writing simple programmes. Nevertheless, he is constantly trying to expand these boundaries. He will innocently ask over dinner, "Mum, is SimCity a creative game?" and when I agree that it probably is, as it asks more of a player than simply fast reflexes, he immediately demands to play it on a computer-free day.

I am beginning to feel that the computer is slowly infiltrating our lives and that it will eventually emerge as a not-so-friendly despot, wielding its authority from the small box bedroom.

It seems a lifetime ago that I naively brought the family a computer for educational purposes, along with a couple of games as light relief between the maths quizzes. Games were simple back then and usually played at the pub between consenting adults after several pints of bitter. Space Invaders and Tennis were the hit favourites at our local. It was only on holiday at the amusement arcades that children were exposed to these seemingly innocent novelties.

Now, however, my son and his peers seem to find just living in the present moment tedious unless it is masked by a Walkman plugged into eager ears, a hand-held computer game or the full fix of the computer terminal punching at full volume. This is supplemented by the ever-active television placed a foot or two from the terminal, so that any transitory moments of boredom, such as when a game is loading up, can be alleviated by a dose of cartoons.

I fear not only that these young people are becoming unfit from lack of exercise but that the involvement in these games is so intense that it results in high levels of stress. I have occasionally found my son flushed and shaking after an especially tense game – and particularly after competing against a friend.

No matter how often I explain to him my feelings about this – and he does appear to understand my anxieties about his health – the bottom line is, he has so much fun with this thing. His eyes come alive when he relates the intricacies and cheats of a new game, and his friendships seem to be enriched through it. These days it is not who is the best centre-forward in the school team but the computer games wizard who is king, and my son is fighting for that crown.

© The Guardian

Glossary

1 cold turkey: a bad reaction felt after a drug is taken away from a drug addict
2 under our feet: in our way
3 adrenaline rush: sudden thrill or excitement
4 Lemmings and Sim City: new computer games
5 moveable feasts: dates or times which can be changed
6 hooked into: absorbed or excited by
7 wielding its authority: controlling us
8 back then: in those days
9 Space Invaders and Tennis: old computer games
10 bitter: a brown beer with a bitter taste
11 our local: our favourite local pub
12 fix: pleasure, thrill, excitement
13 the bottom line: the most important thing

2 As you read, match the words from the article 1–7 with their meanings a–g.

1 enriched   a) came to an agreement to keep everyone happy
2 muttering   b) red in the face from excitement
3 grunt   c) made better or richer
4 compromised   d) entering secretly
5 flushed   e) it doesn't matter how
6 infiltrating   f) speaking in a low, unclear way
7 no matter how   g) a sound made by pigs and some tennis players

3 Now choose the best answer.

a Carolyn Roden ...
 (1) forced her son to give up the computer for a while.
 (2) found it difficult to cope with her son's behaviour.
 (3) only allows him to play computer games one day a week.
b When her son gave up computer games, he ...
 (1) got very bored.
 (2) played a lot of sport.
 (3) spent a lot of time sleeping.
c According to the article, computer games ...
 (1) can be creative but are intense.
 (2) don't require any skill.
 (3) used to be very complicated.
d Carolyn says that computer games ...
 (1) help children to get fit.
 (2) help her son to relax.
 (3) can cause a lot of stress.
e Carolyn's son...
 (1) watches cartoons when the computer is turned off.
 (2) doesn't have any friends.
 (3) appreciates that his mother is worried.

4 Now discuss the following.

a Do you think Carolyn's son is addicted to computer games? Or is he just passionate about his hobby?
b What effect are these games having on her son? Are there any benefits to computer games?
c Is there any difference between an addiction to computer games and an addiction to cigarettes, alcohol or shopping?
d Do you know anyone who is addicted to something? What effect does it have on them? How does it change them?
e Is there anything you would find hard to give up? Why/Why not?

5 Divide into two groups.

Group 1
a With your partners, invent a character who is addicted to something. Imagine how they would describe their addiction and write some notes together. Here are some ideas for addictions.

| alcohol   shopping   cleaning and tidying the house |
| drugs   soap operas   football   cigarettes |

b Choose one person in the group to role play the addict to the rest of the class. Use the following useful language.

My name is ... I am addicted to ...
My addiction has changed my life in many ways.
For example, ...
Every day, I ...
When I take my 'drug', I feel ... . Without it, I feel ...
In the future, I hope that ... . That's my story.
Now are there any questions you would like to ask me about my addiction?

Group 2
a With your partners, think of ways that you can help people overcome an addiction. Here are some ideas.

| take up a new hobby   join a club   play more sport |
| meet new friends   go on holiday   see a doctor |

b Ask the person in group 1 any questions you can think of and use the following useful language.

Why don't you ...
Have you thought of ...?
You really should ...
You must/mustn't ...
If I were you, I'd ...

8 Glasses for your dog

What can you do if your dog has poor eyesight and cannot see very well? A group of American scientists have now come up with a simple solution. They have invented Doggles, special glasses for dogs with poor vision.

1 Before you read, discuss the following.
What do you think of dogs wearing glasses?
Is it sensible and practical, or strange and unnatural?

For the pet whose sight has gone to the dogs

BY DAVID WILES

If your dog no longer recognises the postman or insists on barking up the wrong tree, help is in sight.

Pets whose world has gone fuzzy could find a clearer view with a pair of canine spectacles.

Doggles, as they are called, are strapped in place and look a little like aviator goggles.

The Californian company that produces them has a range of colours to ensure dogs look like the cat's whiskers (as well as being able to see them).

Before buying, owners take their pets to a vet for an eye test. The test involves using a retinoscope, a torch-like instrument which examines the inside of the eye by shining a light through the pupil to the retina. Some of the light bounces back – similar to the flash in a cat's eye when caught in a car's headlight.

As the retinoscope is moved, the returning light moves too, allowing the vet to decide the level of correction needed.

Opthalmologists use a similar technique when testing children too young to read an eye chart.

The company behind Doggles, Midknight Creation, hopes they will bring an end to the days when poor-sighted dogs had only their sense of smell to help them navigate their way around.

'People love their dogs and would do anything for them – they are really going to go for this,' said owner Ken DiLullo.

Doggles, which cost about £40 a pair, will be stocked in pet shops and can be ordered on the Internet.

Dr Michael Brinkman, a veterinary ophthalmologist in Las Vegas who helped develop the idea, said he was testing the glasses on some of his patients.

He said the biggest problem was getting dogs to wear them without trying to pull them off. But he was confident they could be trained to get used to them. Dr Brinkman said the glasses could be used to correct the farsightedness that occurs in dogs that have had cataract surgery but could not have lens implants.

He said: 'A dog that has undergone cataract surgery without receiving a lens implant will be able to spot a cat across the street but perhaps not see a piece of biscuit in front of its food dish.'

© Daily Mail

NEWSPAPER ARTICLES TO GET TEENAGERS TALKING Moral issues

Glossary

1 gone to the dogs: an idiom meaning become really bad
2 barking up the wrong tree: an expression meaning looking in the wrong place
3 in sight: coming soon, on its way
4 Doggles: a trade word made by combining dogs and goggles (the protective glasses you wear for skiing, swimming under water etc.)
5 the cat's whiskers: an old-fashioned idiom meaning really good, the best, fantastic

2 As you read, complete the crossword with ten words from the text. The correct answers will reveal the name of another word for glasses.

Clues
1 Dogs have a great _____ of smell.
2 a part of the eye or a student at school
3 an animal doctor
4 Doggles come in a range of _____ .
5 the end is in _____ (=approaching, coming soon)
6 a loud, aggressive noise made by a dog
7 belonging to the dog family or like a dog
8 You switch these on when you drive at night.
9 found at the back of the eye
10 make sure, guarantee

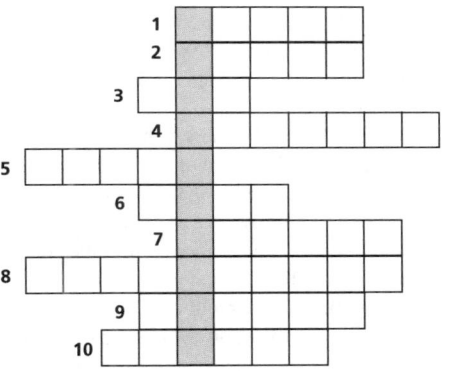

3 Now circle T (True) or F (False).

a The Doggles are held in place by a strap. T / F
b Doggles only come in one colour. T / F
c Dogs have an eye test before their owners buy the Doggles. T / F
d The retinoscope is a kind of torch. T / F
e The retina is in front of the pupil. T / F
f Mr DiLullo thinks Doggles will be a big success. T / F
g You can only buy Doggles on the internet. T / F
h Dr Brinkman helped to create the glasses. T / F
i Dogs take to the Doggles straight away. T / F

4 Rearrange the words below to make seven common idioms, then explain what the expressions mean.

a me, / my / dog / love / love
b raining / it's / and / dogs / cats
c lie / let / dogs / sleeping
d teach / can't / tricks / dog / old / an / new / you
e life / a / dog's / it's
f has / day / every / its / dog
g friend / dog / best / is / man's / a / a

5 Now discuss the following.

a What are the most common pets in your country? Do you have a pet?
b Why are pets so popular? What sort of people like pets?
c What are the best/worst things about having pets?
d Do animals have rights? If so, what sort of rights do they have?
e Which of the following do you think is a good idea?

> stop eating meat   close down zoos
> ban all kinds of hunting and fishing
> stop all medical experiments on animals

6 Your group have been asked to interview members of the public for a radio programme called *Me and my pet*.

a Write the interviews (about a minute long). The pet owners can be people you know, or imaginary characters. The pets can be conventional or unconventional. Use the following language.

Could you introduce yourself and tell us about your pet?
My name is _____ and I have a _____ called _____ who is _____ years old.
I really love my _____ because _____
Is it easy looking after a _____ ?
Well, a typical day with _____ would be like this.
In the morning, _____
In the afternoon _____, and then in the evening _____. At weekends, _____
What's the best thing about having a pet like this?
For me, it's _____

b Choose one person to be the interviewer. The others play the pet owners.
c Act out the interviews for the rest of the class, adding any sound effects that might be appropriate!

9 Helping the homeless

FROM A CONSUL HOUSE

Mrs Naysmith's old home.

TO AN ESTATELY HOME
Bag lady evicted from Ford is given a Merc

BY PAUL THOMPSON

A BAG lady evicted from a Ford Consul where she lived for 20 years moved into a new home yesterday – a Mercedes estate.

Ann Naysmith was left in tears when council chiefs ordered her rusty Consul to be towed away.

But neighbour Sian Lin came to the rescue – and gave delighted Ann her family's old red Merc.

Sian and other caring neighbours parked the Merc in the same spot her Consul had occupied, and even decorated it with flowers and a welcome card.

Council chiefs in Chiswick, West London, said they had towed away Ann's Consul from the posh road where it was parked because they were worried over her health. But pals say officials acted because some residents complained the eyesore car was hitting property prices in the street, where homes fetch more than £500,000.

The council had allocated a flat for Ann to move into after her car was towed away – but she refused to go.

Grateful

Neighbour Sian, 40 – an actress who has appeared in Casualty, EastEnders and The Bill – said: "We had no option really but to give her a new car.

"She is part of the community round here and didn't deserve to be treated like that."

Ann, once an acclaimed pianist, moved into the Ford Consul after she was evicted from a house in the same road when it was redeveloped by the landlord in the '80s.

She grows vegetables in a tiny plot and cooks on a makeshift barbecue in a nearby car park.

Ann appeared grateful for her new home yesterday but said her priority was to get back her Consul.

She insisted: "This is only a stopgap overnight. I am going to fight to make the council put my own car back there where it belongs. They should never have removed it in the first place. It was not doing anyone any harm."

Considerate neighbours covered the Merc's windows with paper to give Ann some privacy and even put a Frank Sinatra tape in the motor to give her something to listen to.

Sian's husband Kit, also 40, said: "Miss Naysmith is the most extraordinarily considerate and scrupulous person I have ever met."

Fellow neighbour, Sally Warren, 46 said: "This is a partial success but we are still determined to get Miss Naysmith's car back. We are going to do whatever it takes."

But just hours after Ann moved in, her new "motor home" was slapped with a £30 parking fine for not showing a pay-and-display ticket.

The council said the warden had been despatched after it received a complaint about the Merc. But a neighbour pal of Ann's accused council officials of being vindictive.

The chum said: "The wardens used to leave the old Consul alone, but her Mercedes is here for a matter of hours and they issue a ticket. They are just trying to force her to leave."

© The Sun

NEWSPAPER ARTICLES TO GET TEENAGERS TALKING Moral issues

On pages 24 and 26 you will read about homeless people. The first article is about a 60-year-old homeless woman called Ann Naysmith. When Ann was younger, she was a famous pianist, but then she had problems with money and ended up living in a rusty old car parked on a street in a wealthy part of London called Chiswick.

 Before you read, discuss the following.

How do you think the residents of the street feel about Ann?

Glossary

1 FROM A CONSUL HOUSE TO AN ESTATELY HOME: Tabloid newspapers love using puns in their headlines. The joke here is based on a play on words. A consul and an estate are types of car, but a council house is a property owned by the local government and a stately home is a huge private aristocratic house
2 bag lady: a homeless woman who carries all her possessions in a bag
3 fetch: are sold for
4 makeshift: improvised
5 Casualty, EastEnders, The bill: Popular TV programmes
6 a stopgap: a temporary solution

 As you read, match A and B to understand words from the article.

A	B
1 If a person is evicted from a property, they ...	a ... your friends.
2 If you tow a car away, you ...	b ... a small piece of land.
3 When a car is rusty ...	c ... are cruel and looking for revenge.
4 A posh area is ...	d ... move it using a rope or chain.
5 An eyesore is ...	e ... the metal is reddish-brown.
6 A plot is ...	f ... are forced to leave.
7 If you are vindictive, you ...	g ... an ugly thing in an inappropriate place.
8 A scrupulous person is ...	h ... gave Mrs Naysmith a parking ticket.
9 Your chums and your pals are ...	i ... honest and trustworthy.
10 A traffic warden ...	j ... wealthy and upper-class.

Now circle T (True) or F (False).

a Ann Naysmith lived in the Ford Consul for 30 years.   T / F
b Council chiefs cried when she was evicted.   T / F
c The Mercedes is in the same parking space as the Ford.   T / F
d Some residents say that Ann's car is effecting property prices.   T / F
e Ann did not want to move into a council flat.   T / F
f Ann was once a very good pianist.   T / F
g She buys her food from the local supermarket.   T / F
h Ann wants her old car back.   T / F
i Sally Warren wants Ann to leave.   T / F
j The council said some people did not want the Mercedes to be there.   T / F

Now read the next article about homeless people.

THE POLICE HAVE A DUTY TO EVERY HOUSEHOLDER

Matthew's 21 and has been living in a 'bash' for six months. His parents don't know where he is. His girlfriend, Nicky, is younger and three months pregnant.

The 'bash' is built from planks and crates, roofed with old rugs and plastic sheeting and raised off the ground with wooden pallets. The nearest running water is in a nearby church hall. There's no electricity.

Matthew and Nicky don't go hungry. A mobile kitchen brings soup and rolls every night. Students from King's College, across the river, regularly bring food. On the face of it – a brave face – they wouldn't give up this life for anything.

They don't bother with the dole. Matthew candidly says that it's a waste of time when they can make do by begging in the West End.

It's this that brings them into conflict with us. Matthew talks about Paul and Charlie, both officers at nearby Kennington Road Police Station.

"Paul's caught me begging once, he gave me a warning," Matthew says. "But if he catches me again he'll do me."

Paul puts the other point of view. "Some people think the Vagrancy Act is obsolete and should be scrapped. But while it's there, we have to enforce it. And we have to think of the nuisance to other people."

Indeed, most commuters find the beggars and their dogs frightening. Many think the police should evict the vagrants and clear away the 'bashes'.

But the fact is that we owe a duty to these citizens too. Our real work with the 'bashdwellers' is not the cat and mouse game of trying to catch them with their palms out. It's the work the public never see: helping to get someone a hospital bed. Encouraging those who need to visit drug and alcohol rehabilitation centres.

Directing newly homeless people to hostels and free kitchens. Putting our heads together with social workers, housing officers, welfare and benefits offices and voluntary organisations.

It's spending hours talking to homeless people finding out about their lives and their problems. Where they've come from. If their families know where they are. And persuading the young ones to return home.

"We'll try to give them the respect that every Londoner is entitled to," Paul says.

Partly as a result of his help, Nicky and Matthew have reached the end of their life on the road. They're moving to a flat before their baby is born.

Reading this you may be in local government, a social worker, architect, counsellor, teacher, or anyone with an interest in the plight of the homeless.

If you would like to know more about how we can work together to ease the problems of homelessness, please call the Metropolitan Police **0800 662244**.

© Metropolitan Police

Every night in London, hundreds of people sleep outside, using shop doorways, park benches or even the pavement for a 'bed'. Under the railway arches near Waterloo train station, rough sleepers have built temporary shelters called 'bashes' made of wood and plastic. In this newspaper advert, the London police (known as the Metropolitan Police) talk about their work with the people who live in the 'bashes'.

4 Before you read, discuss the following.
How do you think the police and the residents of the 'bashes' get on?

Glossary

1 pallet: a rough, wooden platform
2 a mobile kitchen: a food stall run by a charity
3 to put on a brave face: to pretend everything is OK when it is not
4 the dole: money paid to people who are unemployed
5 to make do: to survive, to manage, to just get by
6 the West End: an area of London famous for its theatres
7 he'll do me: he will punish me/he will arrest me
8 the Vagrancy Act: the laws about begging and homelessness
9 bashdwellers: people who live in the bashes
10 with their palms out: begging
11 putting our heads together: discussing and trying to solve a problem

5 As you read, match the words from the article 1–10 with their meanings a–j.

1	crates	a)	very old fashioned, out of date
2	rug	b)	has a right to
3	on the face of it	c)	remove, take away
4	obsolete	d)	large, wooden boxes
5	scrapped	e)	someone who gives help and advice
6	evict	f)	desperate, difficult situation
7	rehabilitation	g)	apparently
8	is entitled to	h)	cancelled, got rid of
9	counsellor	i)	a kind of small carpet
10	plight	j)	helping people find their way back into society

6 Now complete the sentences with information from the article.

a Matthew's girlfriend Nicky is three months _____ .
b Their 'bash' is made of planks and crates covered with _____ and _____ sheeting.
c There is no electricity or running _____ in the 'bash'.
d Matthew and Nicky eat _____ and _____ from a mobile kitchen every night.
e Students from King's College often bring them _____ too.
f They do not apply for the dole because they get enough money by _____ .
g Some _____ are afraid of the beggars and their dogs.
h Rehabilitaion centres help people who have problems with _____ and _____ .
i Paul says that every Londoner is entitled to _____ .
j Matthew and Nicky will be living in a _____ when their baby is born.

7 Now discuss the following.

a Are there many homeless people in your country? Where do they sleep? How do they survive?
b Why do people become homeless, do you think?
c What do you feel when you see someone begging? Do you feel sad or angry?
d Do you give them money or walk on by?
e Are you frightened by beggars? Should begging be banned?
f What can we do to make the situation better for homeless people?

8 Your local radio station is doing a programme about homelessness. They have asked you to interview someone who sleeps rough to find out how they spend a typical day.

a In pairs, write the interview with the homeless person.
b Now perform the interview for the rest of the class.

10 Compensation culture

In July 1998, 83-year-old Stella Liebeck bought a cup of coffee from her local Macdonald's restaurant. When she went to drink it, the cup slipped and she spilled the boiling coffee onto her lap, burning both her legs. Mrs Liebeck was so angry that she took Macdonald's to court, saying that the restaurant should have warned her that the coffee would be hot. The court agreed and Macdonald's were forced to pay her $1,700,000 in compensation.

1 Before you read, discuss the following.
What do you think of this story?
Whose fault was it, Mrs Liebeck's, Macdonald's or nobody's?
Was $1,700,000 fair compensation for her injuries?

Now read two articles that describe the growing 'compensation culture' in Britain and America. These cases are so common that an internet company now organises the annual Stella Awards (named after Mrs Liebeck), where prizes are given to those who make the most ridiculous compensation claims of the year.

SAFEWAY LEAFLET CRIPPLED MY DOG

Muffin's letter-box injury

SAFEWAY bosses were left with a hefty claim after a DOG hurt itself grabbing a store leaflet posted through the door.

Pet lovers Gordon and Susan Musselwhite say their dachshund Muffin leapt up and fell awkwardly.

They returned home to find the pooch lying motionless in the hallway. The leaflets in the letter-box had teeth marks.

The six-year-old pet dislocated a disc in his spine and needed immediate surgery.

Dad-of-two Gordon said: "It was heartbreaking. Our children have grown up and our dogs are like a second family to us.

"We were warned it would be an expensive operation but what do you do?"

Now the retired couple want £2,300 for vet's fees and legal bills after a two-year legal battle with Safeway. They say the leaflet should have been put in a postbox by their front gate.

CIRCULARS

Gordon, 61, of Yealmpton, Devon said: "We have notices up saying we don't want circulars and a bright red letter-box right by the gate.

"We don't want things through our letterbox because it provokes the dogs. We did not invite anyone on to our property to cause this damage."

Safeway has referred the matter to its insurers. A spokeswoman said: "All complaints are taken very seriously."

© The Sun

Glossary

1 Safeway: a major supermarket chain
2 pooch: dog
3 circular: a printed advertisement delivered to lots of addresses

 2 As you read, complete the crossword with ten words from the text.

Across
1 injured so badly that you cannot walk
4 a woman who speaks on behalf of a company or organisation
5 animal doctor
7 uncomfortably, in a clumsy way, in a way that might cause injury
8 opposite of pale
9 taking forcefully
10 not moving

Down
2 jumped
3 backbone
6 really sad

3 Now circle T (True) or F (False).

a	Safeways put a circular through the Musselwhite's door.	T / F
b	Muffin was hit on the head by the leaflet.	T / F
c	The dog jumped up to try and catch the leaflet.	T / F
d	The Musselwhites were at home when the accident happened.	T / F
e	The dog injured her neck.	T / F
f	Muffin had an operation a few weeks later.	T / F
g	The vet did not tell the family it would be an expensive operation.	T / F
h	Mr Musselwhite is still working.	T / F
i	The Musselwhites have a postbox next to their front door.	T / F
j	Safeways are not interested in the case.	T / F

Now read *Writs a mad, mad world*.

AMERICANS CASH IN WITH CRAZY COURT CLAIMS

Writs a mad, mad world!

CLAIM 1: When convicted bank robber Michael Brodson decided to make a break for freedom by scaling a 40ft prison wall, he ended up falling off and breaking his leg. Brodson promptly sued Ohio prison authorities, claiming they had failed to inform him that climbing the wall was dangerous.
RESULT: *Bradson received £12,000 for his efforts.*

CLAIM 2: Drunk driver Franklin Loadaer was so hammered one night that he went through several detour signs near his Illinois home before crashing his car through a hedge and into a wall.
When he sobered up, he sued the engineering company that designed the road, the contractor, four subcontractors and the state highway department.
RESULT: *After five years of legal wrangling, all of the defendants agreed to make the case go away by settling with Loadaer for £21,000. The engineering firm was left with a legal bill for £120,000.*

CLAIM 3: Teenager Carl Truman sued after his neighbour ran over his hand with a Honda Accord outside his Los Angeles home.
RESULT: *Even Truman must have been surprised to receive a £45,000 pay-out plus medical expenses - considering he had been trying to steal his neighbour's car at the time!*

CLAIM 4: Kathleen Robertson, of Austin, Texas tripped over a toddler in a furniture store.
RESULT: *She won a whopping £470,000 compensation payout - even though the toddler who floored her was Robertson's own son!*

CLAIM 5: They say people can get burned at barbecues... but spare a thought for the friendly neighbour who invited Alan Dunane over for sausages and steak.
After drinking heavily throughout the afternoon Alan, from Florida, climbed on to the back fence and attempted to walk along its length. Instead, he fell off into a canal on the other side and injured himself.
RESULT: *Dunane sued his neighbour because he claimed the fence had a flat top, rather than a pointed one, so he could walk on it. Amazingly, Dunane won the case and received £6,000 compensation.*

CLAIM 6: Merv Grazinski, of Oklahoma purchased a brand new 32ft Winnebago motor home. On his first trip he set the cruise control at 70mph and calmly left the driver's seat as the Winnebago sped along the motorway, to go into the back and make himself a cup of coffee. Not surprisingly, the vehicle left the motorway shortly afterwards and crashed.
RESULT: *Grazinski sued Winnebago for not advising him in the owner's manual that he couldn't actually leave the vehicle to drive itself. The jury awarded him £1,250,000 plus a new motor home.*

CLAIM 7: Delaware clubber Kara Wilson decided to climb in through a nighclub's toilet window to avoid paying the £2 entry fee. She slipped, knocked out her two front teeth on the floor below - and sued.
RESULT: *She was awarded £7,000 and free dental expenses to repair her mangled gnashers.*

CLAIM 8: Sweet-toothed Robert Forster, of Ohio, is currently suing both the manufacturers of M&Ms and his local store for "mislabelled and defective merchandise" after a packet of peanut-flavoured sweets included a plain one.
Forster claim he bit down on the plain one too hard thinking it was a peanut one and cut through the skin on his lip. The injury, he says, then required a visit to the hospital.
RESULT: *The claim is still going through the courts - but if he wins, he stands to get £300,000.*

© The Sunday People

Glossary

1 **writ:** a legal document explaining your claim (in the title, *writs* is a pun on *it's*)
2 **hammered:** very drunk
3 **sobered up:** became sober again (*sober* is the opposite of *drunk*)
4 **wrangling:** long, complicated argument
5 **toddler:** a very young child just learning how to walk
6 **whopping:** very large, huge
7 **floored:** knocked down onto the floor
8 **Winnebago:** a make of motor home
9 **40ft/32ft:** 12.19m/9.75m.
10 **mangled gnashers:** damaged teeth

As you read, answer the questions to find the meaning of these words.

a Does *scaled* mean climbed or fell from?
b Does *promptly* mean very quickly or after some delay?
c Is a *hedge* a barrier made of stone or made from plants/small trees?
d Does *settling with* mean continuing the fight or coming to an agreement?
e Does *purchased* mean sold or bought?
f Does *sped* (the past of *speed*) mean went quickly or went slowly?
g Does *manual* here mean by hand or a kind of book?
h Does *sweet-toothed* refer to someone who enjoys sweet things or someone who hates chocolate?

5 Now write the number of the claim or claims to answer these questions.

In which claim(s) ...

a did the claimant sue a neighbour?
b were the claimants drunk?   ....
c was the claimaint trying to avoid paying?   ....
d was there an injury caused by a fall?   ....
e were drivers involved in a crash?   ....
f was there an accident caused by a very young child?   ....
g did claimants suffer injuries to their mouths?   ....
h did the claimant receive the most compensation?   ....

6 Read and discuss the following statements.

> **Use this useful language.**
> - *How can you blame (someone) if ...?*
> - *People should take more care when they ...*
> - *It all depends on ...*
> - *It's not my/his/the government's fault if ...*
> - *It's a grey area ...*
> - *to take responsibility for ...*
> - *to blame someone else for ...*
> - *over the top (=excessive) ...*
> - *to claim damages (financial compensation) from / for ...*

a Smokers should be able to sue tobacco companies.
b If you do not like a film, the cinema should give you your money back.
c Companies that pollute the atmosphere should be heavily fined.
d If your train, plane or bus is delayed, you should always get compensation.
e If you fail your exams, you should be able to sue your school.
f Africans should get compensation for the slave trade of 200 years ago.
g An actress photographed shopping without her make-up should be able to sue any paper that prints the pictures.
h People who drop litter or chewing gum should pay for it to be picked up.

Imagine you are one of the characters in the newspaper articles. Write your claim for compensation, then present it to the class.

> *My name is ...*
>
> *I am here today to claim ... from ... because I ...*
>
> *What happened was ...*
>
> *It wasn't my fault because ...*
>
> *You should award me the money because ...*

Let the class ask you questions, then have a class vote to see if the claim is successful or not. Is your class's decision the same as the decision taken by the courts?

11 Free money

One evening in April 2004, the villagers of Wooler in the north of England discovered that the cash machine outside their local bank was giving away free money. If you asked for £20, the machine gave you £40. If you asked for £100, it gave you £200. In fact, every customer was getting twice as much money as they had asked for.

1 Before you read, discuss the following.
The machine was full of cash and all the bank staff had gone home. What do you think happened over the next ten hours?

Villagers strike it rich as they discover cash machine is doubling their money

BY AUSLAN CRAMB
AND PAUL STOKES

THE villagers of Wooler were still wearing broad smiles yesterday as they fondly recalled Golden Wednesday. It was only seven days ago, but it was "the busiest night of the year," and they will be talking about it for years to come.

It was the night the Barlcays Bank cash machine in the Northumberland village paid out twice as much money as every customer asked for. News travels fast in rural communities and within an hour there was a queue the length of the High Street. One woman arrived at the machine by taxi, in her nightdress.

The residents of Wooler (pop. 2,000) quickly realised they could use all their dedit cards in the machine, and that if they asked for £200 they would receive £400.

The extraordinary bonanza was caused by the replacement at about 9pm last Wednesday, by staff from Securicor, of a cassette that contained £10 notes with one containing £20 notes.

In the two pubs across the road, the talk was of some locals making "thousands of pounds" from the error.

And it quickly occurred to those who had made a withdrawal that they could return after midnight – the start of a new banking day – and do the same again.

As if queueing for a prize item in the January sales, they began to wait in line once more before midnight.

Within hours the machine had been emptied, and it was estimated in the village that at least £65,000 had been withdrawn.

The rumour mill suggested pubs had stayed open late to make the most of it, but it was difficult to find anyone who admitted to profiting from the incident.

The landlady of the Angel pub who asked not to be named, expressed disappointment that she had not joined in the windfall, adding: "If only I could have remembered my PIN number."

She insisted it had not been unusually busy in the pub, although outside it had been "the busiest night in Wooler for years.

"There were people coming from all over the place, from Powburn, Millfield and Lowick. It wasn't just the people from Wooler," she added. "This is a great place for rumours, and it wasn't long before everybody knew about it.

"Some people didn't go because they thought they would get into trouble, or would have to hand the money back, and I heard that someone went into the bank the next day and handed over the extra money she got."

Next door at the Black Bull pub, there was astonishment yesterday at the news that Barclays would not be asking customers to return their bonus payments.

A spokesman for the bank said it was a "third-party error. Our policy is that we will get back to whoever caused the error in the first place and ask them to compensate us for the loss," he said.

Whoever was to blame, the general view in Wooler was that "the banks rob you blind anyway, this is just small change to them but a lot of money to us".

© The Daily Telegraph

NEWSPAPER ARTICLES TO GET TEENAGERS TALKING Moral issues

Glossary

1 Barclays: one of Britain's biggest banks
2 Northumberland: a county in the north of England
3 pop: an abbreviation for population
4 Securicor: a security firm that loads cash into cashpoint machines
5 PIN: Personal Identification Number, the security number you use to withdraw cash
6 Powburn, Millfield and Lowick: neighbouring villages

2 As you read, match the words from the article 1–7 with their meanings a–h.

1 broad
2 rural area
3 it occurred to them
4 windfall
5 astonishment
6 rob you blind
7 confessed

a) take everything from you
b) admitted
c) great surprise
d) very wide
e) they suddenly realised that
f) sudden, unexpected bonus
h) countryside

3 Now circle T (True) or F (False).

a One woman came to the cashpoint wearing a nightdress. T / F
b The Angel and The Black Bull are close to the bank. T / F
c Some people made more than one withdrawal. T / F
d About £5,000 was taken from the machine. T / F
e The landlady of the Angel pub did not want to make any withdrawals. T / F
f People from nearby villages joined in too. T / F
g Nobody handed the extra cash back to the bank. T / F
h The bank will ask customers to repay the money. T / F
i Most of the villagers feel guilty about what happened. T / F

4 Now discuss the following.

a Were the residents of Wooler right to keep the extra money?
b An English proverb suggests that 'Honesty is the best policy'. Do you agree or disagree?
c Do you always tell people the truth? Or are there times when a 'white lie' is a kinder, better thing to do?

5 Find out how honest your classmates are. In groups, answer the following.

a A friend offers you some pirate CDs at half the usual price. Do you ...
  (1) buy them?
  (2) get angry and look for a new friend?
  (3) laugh and ask her how much money she is making?

b You find a mobile phone on a park bench. Do you ...
  (1) leave it on the bench?
  (2) use it to make some long distance calls?
  (3) take it to a police station?

c Your best friend leaves his diary at your house. Do you ...
  (1) read it?
  (2) have a quick look to see what he says about you?
  (3) give it back to him the next day unopened?

d You want a new camera. Do you ...
  (1) get a part-time job and save up the money?
  (2) tell the insurance company your old one has been stolen?
  (3) go shoplifting in a store?

e You find an envelope marked 'tomorrow's exam: secret' near the school staff room. Do you ...
  (1) photocopy the exam and sell copies to your friends?
  (2) memorise the questions and re-seal the envelope?
  (3) take it to the staff room unopened and study hard for the test?

f In a restaurant, the waiter gives you a bill for £5 instead of £20. Do you ...
  (1) pay £5 and leave quickly?
  (2) pay £5 but leave him a big tip?
  (3) point out the mistake and ask for a new bill?

Discuss your answers. What do they say about you?

What makes some people dishonest? Can you think of a job or situation where being dishonest may be an advantage?

12 Starting again

The man who swapped lives

Alistair with his second wife.

Alistair Liddle had his own law firm and seemed happily married. So why did he disappear off the face of the earth?
By Natalie Clarke

One hot summer's day, a tall, slim man with close-cropped red hair drove into the small Scottish town of Forres and parked outside the offices of a law firm called Liddle & Co.

He knew many of the locals walking past, but they did not recognise him. Hardly surprising considering many thought that the man – lawyer Alistair Liddle – had died four years ago.

Back then he'd been one of the town's most respected residents. As well as running a law firm he was chairman of the Round Table and a regular at the local golf club.

Then, just before Christmas 1997, he kissed his wife of 18 years goodbye, set off for a meeting and never came back. While police hunted for his body and his picture appeared on BBC1's Crimewatch, he was busy setting up a new life 800 miles away.

And had it not been for an unlucky chance, Alistair Liddle would probably have remained missing, presumed dead, to this day. His true identity was only revealed when he was questioned by police on an entirely unrelated murder enquiry.

He later served six months behind bars for embezzling funds from his business to pay for his new life. And it was on his way home from prison that he stopped off in his old home town.

"It was weird," he says, "but I couldn't resist having a look around. No one recognised me, which is probably just as well."

Home today is a cottage in Penzance, where he lives with his new partner, Paula, 40, her daughter Janine, 11, and their own 18-month-old daughter, Iona.

Explaining why he felt the need to do a bunk, he says: "My home life was intolerable. My wife's mother would come to visit for a day and end up staying for weeks. I felt she detested me."

Alistair, 43, met his wife, Annamarie, on a school trip when they were kids. But after two decades together, they had drifted apart. "We had nothing to say to each other. I used to enjoy going out, but my wife preferred to stay at home. It got to the point where we couldn't stand the sight of one another," he says.

As well as his marriage hitting the rocks, his business was in trouble. "I was having serious problems balancing the books and couldn't see a way out of it. Clients weren't paying on time and I was getting more and more into debt." Alistair became increasingly stressed and began hitting the bottle, later being accused of drink driving. By now his weight had ballooned to 20st.

"I was this pillar of the community and couldn't face the disgrace. I was seriously considering suicide as the only way out. But then I read a newspaper article about someone who'd gone missing and started a new life, and it got me thinking."

The day before he disappeared, Alistair went Christmas shopping with his wife. The next day he told her he was going to a Law Society meeting in Edinburgh and would return later that evening. He never came home.

Instead, he boarded a train to York, where he stayed in a hotel for a few days under a false name, cutting his hair and shaving off his moustache.

"I was relieved," he says. "Feeling guilty was the last thing on my mind. I didn't feel bad about my wife."

He even left his widowed mother wondering if he was dead or alive. "I couldn't send her a card saying I was OK, because then I could be traced. I did feel guilty about upsetting her but there was nothing I could do."

His distraught wife filed a missing persons report with police, who searched fields for a body. Posters showing Alistair's face popped up everywhere.

Meanwhile, the man himself worked his way to Penzance, picking daffodils for £50 a day. The weight fell off him and he went down to 13st.

Rob Fox, as he had named himself – Rob after Rob Roy, Fox in homage to what he saw as his own cunning – was beginning to forget all about the old Alistair Liddle. Until a local murder took place and he was caught up in the manhunt. Although not involved in any way, he gave them a false address when interviewed.

It was a foolish mistake. When the details were checked, everything fell into place. Alistair had never paid his £300 drink-drive fine and was promptly taken in handcuffs back to Scotland.

His astonished wife was informed that her husband was alive, but she declined an offer by the police to visit him in his cell. And who could blame her? While Alistair had been picking flowers in the Cornish sunshine, her home had been repossessed.

On Alistair's first date with widow Paula Pirie, who he met in a Cornwall nightclub, he admitted his secret double life. "I wanted to come clean immediately, so she could take me for what I was or call the whole thing off," he explained.

Paula gave him a chance, saying: "I found him funny, kind and easygoing – quite charming."

In January 2000, Alistair was charged with embezzlement and pleaded guilty to stealing £17,870. "I did something wrong and I paid the price," he says. "I hated being a lawyer anyway. I take things at a slower pace now. I don't miss anything about my old life."

© The News of the World

This is an amazing, true story about a Scottish lawyer called Alistair Liddle. At the age of 43, Alistair had a mid-life crisis. One day, he told his wife he was going to a meeting. Then he got on a train and just disappeared. He never contacted his friends or family to tell them what he was doing (they thought he was dead) and he started a completely new life 800 miles away, with a new name and a new job.

1 Before you read, discuss the following.
What is a mid-life crisis?
Why do people sometimes want to completely change their life, or their clothes, appearance and lifestyle?
Do you know anyone who has done this?

Glossary

1 the Round Table: an organisation that raises funds for local charities
2 Crimewatch: a TV programme that asks the public to help solve crimes
3 to do a bunk: to run away (usually breaking the law in the process)
4 balancing the books: ensuring the business income can pay for the outgoings
5 Rob Roy: a legendary Scottish freedom fighter
6 20st: 20 stone (127kg)

2 As you read, answer the questions to find the meaning of these words.

a Does *close-cropped* mean very short or very long?
b Does *setting up* mean starting or finishing?
c Does *behind bars* mean being in pubs or in prison?
d If something is *just as well*, is it lucky or unlucky?
e Is *hitting the rocks* getting into trouble or getting stronger?
f Is *hitting the bottle* drinking heavily or giving up alcohol?
g Does *ballooned* mean increased gradually or increased quickly?
h Is *a pillar of the community* someone who is well respected or hated?
i Does *popped up* mean appeared or disappeared?
j Does *come clean* mean have a wash or admit the truth?

3 Now circle T (True) or F (False).

a Alistair Liddle spent a year in prison. T / F
b He now lives in a cottage in Edinburgh. T / F
c Annamarie was his childhood sweetheart. T / F
d When his business failed, he began drinking heavily. T / F
e He phoned his mother to tell her he was safe. T / F
f He lost a lot of weight while picking flowers. T / F
g He used a false name to hide his identity. T / F
h The police took him back to Scotland. T / F
i Annamarie came to see him in prison. T / F
j He met his second wife at a nightclub. T / F
k He decided to tell Paula the truth straight away. T / F
l Alistair wishes he could go back to his old life again. T / F

4 Now discuss the following.

a Do you think Alistair Liddle was brave or selfish?
b His second wife, Paula, says he deserves a second chance. Do you agree with her?
c Should you always do what you want in life? Or is being selfish always bad?
d Is it possible to live your life for other people, and not to think of yourself?

5 Imagine you are the four main characters in the article. In groups of four, act out a meeting between the characters. Plan what to say first.

My name is Alistair Liddle. I feel so much better now because ...

My name is Annamarie Liddle. Will I ever forgive you, Alistair? Well, I ...

I'm Alistair's mother. When you disappeared, Alistair, I felt ...

My name is Paula Pirie. When I met Alistair, I ...

NEWSPAPER ARTICLES TO GET TEENAGERS TALKING | Moral issues

13 Money matters

On pages 37 and 39, there are two very different articles about wealthy people. First, read about businessman Tom Monaghan. In 1960, he borrowed $900 and started a pizza delivery company. When he sold the business 40 years later, he was one of the richest men in the world and was worth more than $1,000,000,000. But instead of keeping his money in the bank, he decided to give most of it away and spend his time working for charity.

1 Before you read, discuss the following.
Why do you think Tom Monaghan wanted to give away most of his money?

Glossary

1 endeavours: activities
2 the Republican Party: one of the leading political parties in the USA
3 a seminary: a college for people training to be priests
4 the Marine Corps: the US navy
5 prompting: causing, triggering, starting

2 As you read, answer the questions to find the meaning of these words.

a If you *devote* time, do you give it or take it away?
b Does *virtually* mean everything or almost all?
c Is a *host of* one or many?
d Does *renunciation* mean abandoning or embracing?
e Does *reflecting on* mean ignoring or thinking about?
f Is *a stake* a piece of meat or a share in the company?
g Is *a backer* an opponent or a supporter?
h Does *drifting* mean moving to your target or having no real direction?
i Does *enlisted* mean joined or left?
j Does *discharged* mean released or asked to pay money?

3 Now complete the sentences with information from the article.

a Tom Monaghan is selling his collection of vintage _____ .
b He has also sold the _____ team he owned in Chicago.
c He now plans to build a series of _____ schools across America.
d His brother _____ his half-share in the business for a car.
e Their first pizza store was in _____ .
f The brothers borrowed $ _____ to start the business.
g There are now _____ Domino outlets across the globe.
h Tom grew up in a number of _____ homes and an _____ before entering a seminary.
i After leaving the seminary, he joined the _____ .
j His opposition to _____ led some people to boycott Domino's.

4 Rearrange the words to make five proverbs about money.

a on / trees / money / doesn't / grow
   Money doesn't grow on trees.
b money / time / is
c love / money / buy / can't / you
d talks / money
e and / soon / money / fool / his / a / parted / are
f the world / money / go / makes / round

Then explain what each proverb means. Do you agree with them?

Fact file

If you would like to know more about the rich and super rich, you can find all sorts of information on the Forbes Magazine website (www.forbes.com). At the time these two articles were written, the richest people in the world were:
1 Bill Gates (USA) $46,500,000,000
2 Warren Buffett (USA) $44,000,000,000
3 Lakshmi Mittal (India) $25,000,000,000
4 Carlos Slim Helu (Mexico) $23,800,000,000
5 Prince Alwaleed Bin Talal Alsaud
  (Saudi Arabia) $23,700,000,000
6 Ingvar Kamprad (Sweden) $23,000,000,000

Now read about another wealthy person.

Pizza man gives away his millions

By David Sapsted in New York

A SELF-MADE billionaire who created the world's largest home-delivery pizza network has sold up to devote his time – and virtually all his money – to charity.

Tom Monaghan, the founder of Domino's Pizza, has got rid of his helicopter, yacht, aircraft, radio stations, a vintage car collection and an island resort on Lake Huron, dismissing them as "distractions".

The money from those sales has gone to a host of charities, along with $85 million (£50.6 million) from selling the Chicago Cubs baseball team six years ago.

In what the *Wall Street Journal* describes as "an extraordinary renunciation of materialism", Mr Monaghan has now sold more than 90 per cent of his stake in Domino's for $1 billion (£595 million).

"At the age of 61, reflecting on my life and the goals I have yet to fulfil, I have decided to retire from active involvement in Domino's Pizza and devote more time to my charitable endeavours," he said from his home in Ann Arbor, Michigan.

A devout Roman Catholic and backer of the Republican Party, Mr Monaghan has already established a charitable foundation and is expected to spend most of his time and cash in the next few years building Catholic schools across America.

He and his brother James – who swapped his half-share in the business after a year for a Volkswagen Beetle – began their home delivery pizza chain with one Michigan store, DomiNick's, which they bought with $900 (£536) they borrowed in 1960.

Over the years, Mr Monaghan built up the business, concentrating on free, fast home-delivery until the point today when there are 6,100 Domino outlets worldwide, about two-thirds of them in the United States.

Mr Monaghan had a tough childhood, brought up in foster homes and an orphanage before entering a seminary at the age of 17. He stayed there only briefly, drifting aimlessly until he enlisted in the Marine Corps.

When he was discharged, he turned his mind to pizza and, in a fiercely-competitive market, built a chain that is second in size to Pizza Hut.

The entrepreneur also became an opponent of abortion, prompting a boycott of Domino's in America by the National Organisation of Women. Mr Monaghan explained that he had increasingly reflected on his life in recent years. "I realised how bad a person I really am," he said. "It was exciting because it showed I really have got some room for improvement."

He will not be quitting Domino's completely. He retains a small stake and will remain on the board as non-executive chairman.

© The Daily Telegraph

NEWSPAPER ARTICLES TO GET TEENAGERS TALKING Moral issues

In 2003, footballer David Beckham joined the Spanish club Real Madrid and signed a contract worth £120,000 a week. While he and his wife were looking for a new house in Madrid, they stayed in a luxury five-star hotel called the Santo Mauro. After two and a half months, however, they had a shock when the hotel presented them with a bill for £433,000 (606,000 euros).

5 Before you read, discuss the following.
What do you think the Beckhams had spent all that money on?

Glossary

1 valet parking: where hotel staff take care of your car
2 fare: food
3 hit home: had a really powerful effect (on)
4 Newark and JFK: airports in the USA
5 movie moguls: powerful business people in the film industry

6 As you read, match the words from the article 1–10 with their meanings a–j.

1 run up   a) flies
2 astonishing   b) looking everywhere
3 jets   c) very worried
4 revive   d) much loved
5 scouring   e) the opposite of low key; very public
6 alarmed   f) the opposite of high-profile; quiet
7 odd   g) bring back to life
8 beloved   h) occasional
9 high-profile   i) spent (on credit)
10 low-key   j) incredible

7 Now complete the sentences with information from the article.

a The parking charges for his five _____ cars came to _____ .
b The hotel restaurant is open _____ hours a day.
c David prefers to eat _____ food.
d David was _____ when he discovered how much he was spending.
e The bill for 'extras' includes things such as _____ calls, dry _____ and extra _____ to protect their sons Romeo and Brooklyn.
f Romeo had his first _____ party at the hotel this summer.
g David's beloved cars were brought to Spain by _____ .
h Posh Spice is discussing a number of _____ projects in America.
i The couple tried to avoid _____ at the New York airport.
j The Beckhams rented two _____ at the Santo Mauro hotel.

8 Look at the two texts together. Write Beckham, Monaghan or both if there is a reference to the following.

1 a difficult childhood   _Monaghan_
2 cars   _____
3 starting a business   _____
4 food   _____
5 serving in the armed forces   _____
6 alcohol   _____

9 Now discuss the following questions.

> Use this useful language.
> - It's his money, he can do what he likes with it.
> - If I had that kind of money, I would ...
> - The rich get richer and the poor get poorer.
> - It's a rags to riches story. (= when someone is born poor but becomes rich)
> - They're rolling in money. (= very rich)
> - to pour money down the drain (= to waste it)
> - to spend money like water (= spend it very fast, almost without thinking)
> - they're filthy rich (= very rich, slightly derogative)
> - easy come, easy go (= if you earn money easily, you spend it easily)

a What do you spend your money on? If you were David Beckham, would you have spent your money on the same things at the hotel?
b Do you think rich people should give their money to charity, like Tom Monaghan? Or do you think they should spend it to be as comfortable as possible, like David Beckham?
c Do you respect people more if they are rich?
d How does money (or lack of money) change people's lives? What can/can't money buy?

10 Imagine, like Tom Monaghan, you had $1,000,000,000 to give away. In groups, decide what you would do with the money (you cannot give it to yourself or your friends).

a Present your ideas to the rest of the class.
b Have a class vote on the best thing to do.

With Posh away so often, star spends £9,000 watching in-room movies

LONELY BECKHAM RUNS UP A £433,000 HOTEL BILL

By **Mark Reynolds**
Showbusiness Reporter

DAVID Beckham has run up a hotel bill of nearly half a million pounds since moving to Madrid three months ago. The England captain spent £432,875 at the five-star Santo Mauro in just 80 days. Yet only £80,303 of that went on his own accommodation.

Beckham, 28, spent an astonishing £74,285 on valet car parking charges for his five cars.

Another £9,000 went on television and video charges in his two suites.

The midfielder is clearly spending most of his spare time at the Santo Mauro, watching television on his own while his wife Victoria jets to London and New York as she attempts to revive her pop career.

He is also eating many of his meals at the hotel, having spent £54,003 in the restaurant or on room service.

The restaurant is so exclusive it has only seven tables.

A chef is on duty 24 hours a day, ready to cook the player the English fare he prefers.

The Beckhams are still scouring the Spanish capital for a family home suitable for their sons Brooklyn and Romeo, but have so far been unable to agree on a property.

Even Beckham, who is paid £120,000 a week by his new club Real Madrid, was alarmed to learn how much he was spending at the Santo Mauro.

'The bill has hit home,' one friend said last night.

'But the family must be sure all their security and privacy requirements are met. Until then, it is important that David is comfortable.'

Beckham's bill – for 606,025 euros – also included £77,785 on guest rooms for friends, relatives and associates.

His bar bill was a comparatively low £6,857.

While the England captain is not a big drinker, some of his visitors have been enjoying themselves in the bar of the Santo Mauro.

Beckham himself is known to occasionally ask for the odd £36 bottle of wine to be sent up to his suite.

The biggest single item on the bill was £130,642 for extras.

This covered extra security at the 37 bedroom hotel, phone calls, laundry and dry-cleaning charges and Romeo's first birthday party back in the summer.

The huge parking bill is due to Beckham's insistence on having his beloved red Aston Martin, a Porsche, an Audi A8, a gold Lexus and a silver Range Rover shipped over to Madrid following his transfer from Manchester United in July. Earlier this week, the Beckham family flew into Newark Airport for another high-profile visit to the U.S.

The trip was the third in less than a month for the 29-year-old former Posh Spice, who was believed to be meeting movie moguls to discuss 'a number of possible projects'.

They chose a low-key British Airways flight to the New Jersey airport instead of the usual arrival at JFK in an attempt to avoid photographers.

HOTEL ★★★★★
SANTO MAURO

Señor D. Beckham

Accommodation Two luxury suites for 80 nights	**£80,303**
Guest rooms (assorted)	**£77,785**
Parking For choice of five cars shipped from home	**£74,285**
Food English dishes specially prepared by first class chef	**£54,003**
TV/Video Entertainment in Suite	**£9,000**
Bar For string of guests	**£6,857**
Extras Security, laundry Romeo's birthday party phone calls	**£130,642**

TOTAL £432,875

© The Daily Mail

14 Charities

Today: Go for a long drive. Read your children a story. Surf the internet. Catch the barmaid's eye. Fly a kite. Go out bargain hunting. Decorate a room. Weave through a crowd. Whizz around the supermarket. Bid at an auction. Play hide and seek. Change a light bulb. Re-wire a plug. Enjoy an exhibition. Nip across a road and back. Light a barbecue. Give someone directions. Use a vending machine. Ride a bicycle. Fill out a lottery ticket. Put up shelving. Enjoy your favourite view. Follow a recipe. Take a frisbee to the park. Play bingo. Decide on a new hairstyle. Write a cheque. Put in a new hoover bag. Prune your prize roses. Explore somewhere by train. Curl up with a good book. Re-arrange your living room. Flirt with a stranger. Put on a bit of make-up. Tell somebody you think they look nice. Lie under the stars.

Tomorrow: Over a hundred more people like you will start to lose their sight.

RNIB
Helping you live with sight loss
0845 766 9999 www.rnib.org.uk

Registered charity number 226227

© RNIB

NEWSPAPER ARTICLES TO GET TEENAGERS TALKING — Moral issues

There are over 200,000 registered charities in the UK and they all need donations from the public to be able to survive. But with so many good causes competing for people's money, how can a charity get its message across and persuade us to help? In this advertisement, the RNIB (the Royal National Institute of the Blind) adopts a 'soft sell', almost conversational style.

1 Before you read, discuss the following.

What are your favourite charities? What sort of work do they do? How do they raise money from the public?

Glossary

1 weave: move like a snake or slalom skier
2 whizz: go really fast
3 hide and seek: a children's game in which one person hides and the others look for him or her
4 nip across: go quickly, go for a short time
5 curl up: lie down to make yourself comfortable and warm
6 catch someone's eye: get their attention

2 Complete the sentences using these words from the adverts.

| vending | hoover | surf | weaved |
| kite | nip | bargain | bid |

a You use a _____ to clean carpets.
b It's difficult to fly a _____ when the wind is very strong.
c We've got a _____ machine at school that sells soft drinks and snacks.
d The skier _____ her way down the mountain.
e You can _____ the net looking for charity websites.
f I got these lovely earrings at the market. They didn't cost much. They were a _____.
g The team put in a _____ for the football player, but it was not enough money.
h I'm just going to _____ out and get some milk.

3 Find one (or more) phrases in the RNIB advert that refer to …

a travelling
   go for a long drive

b using a computer
   _____

c sports and hobbies
   _____

d shopping
   _____

e making changes to your home
   _____

f trying to win money
   _____

g food
   _____

h flowers
   _____

i reading
   _____

j your appearance
   _____

4 Now discuss the following.

a How does the language of the RNIB advert make you feel about the issue of blindness?
b What would it be like to be blind?
c Do you think it would be a good idea if everyone did a year's charity work or voluntary work after they leave school?
d What are the most important charities in the world? What do they do? Do they really make a difference?

5 Your group have been asked to develop a newspaper advert for a local charity. Decide which charity you will be working for. Then consider the following.

a Who will the advert be aimed at?
b What style will you adopt? Will it be the 'soft sell' approach of the RNIB advert? Or will it be a 'hard sell' approach, using stronger or even shocking language to get your message across?
c What message do you want to get across? Are you trying to raise money or raise awareness?
d How can you grab the attention of the reader? Will you use a simple slogan or a longer text full of information?

Now write, design and draw the advert. Make some rough drafts, then do a final copy to show to the rest of the class. As you present your ad, explain the thinking behind it and ask for feedback.

15 Disciplining children

Mary Marsh of the NSPCC (Britain's main children's charity) says: "It should be as wrong to hit a child as an adult". However, in a recent survey in the UK, 83% of parents said that children needed to be smacked sometimes and that smacking was good for a child. This article looks at the pros and cons of smacking.

1 Before you read, discuss the following.
Were you smacked as a child? If so, how did you feel? Should parents be allowed to smack their children?

Glossary

1 bring into line: discipline
2 behind the times: old fashioned
3 give in: surrender
4 it never crossed my mind to: I never thought of
5 cool off: calm down
6 got away with murder: were never punished whatever they did
7 make up: become friends again

Fact file
- Smacking is banned in many countries.
- In England and Wales, you can legally give your child 'a light smack', but you can be jailed if you leave a bruise, a scratch or a cut on the child's skin.

2 As you read, match the words from the article 1–8 with their meanings a–h.

1	outlawed	a)	promised
2	escalate	b)	hit (usually softly with your hand)
3	dreadful	c)	hit hard
4	vowed	d)	get worse
5	childproof	e)	out of control
6	slap	f)	safe for children to use
7	thump	g)	really bad
8	out of hand	h)	forbidden, made illegal

Further information
The NSPCC (the National Society for the Prevention of Cruelty to Children) website is *www.NSPCC.org.uk*.

3 The sentences below are summaries of what people say in the article. Write who says these points: 'Alice', 'Claire' or 'both'.

a If you're angry, leave the room to calm down. *Alice*
b I would not smack a child who is ten years old. _____
c Make your home a safe and secure environment for a child. _____
d I worked as a nanny for parents who let their children do too many naughty things. _____
e Give your child a warning before you smack them. _____
f I'm not soft on discipline. _____
g You can't reason with very young children. _____
h A small smack can soon become a hard hit. _____
i A smack defuses the tension. _____
j Don't take your frustration out on a child. _____

4 Now discuss the following.

a Who do you agree with, Alice or Claire?
b Do you think violence always leads to more violence?
c Should parents be sent to prison if they smack their children, especially if they leave a bruise or a cut?
d If you had children (or young brothers and sisters), what rules and boundaries would you set them?

5 Your group have been asked to take part in a United Nations debate about the rights of children. At the end of the discussion, the UN will draw up a ten-point Children's Charter.

a In your group, come up with bullet points to complete these sentences.

- We should teach children to ...
- We shouldn't teach children to ...
- A child has a right to ...
- A child has a right not to ...

b Share your ideas with the rest of the class.
c Now vote for the ten best suggestions.

Should smacking ban get backing?

Most mothers believe the best way to discipline a naughty child is with a sharp smack. But this way of bringing kids into line could be banned.

Five European countries including Norway and Sweden have already outlawed smacking. Germany and Scotland are also considering a ban. So are we way behind the times and should we find other ways to discipline children?

Child experts have mixed views. Penelope Leach, author of best-selling *Baby and Child*, campaigns with anti-smacking group EPOCH.

She says "Children learn from example and every time you smack your child you tell him that aggression is okay.

"We all want our children to be self-disciplined but that comes through setting good examples not through endless punishment. The rule is to say no and mean it."

Lynette Burrows, mother of six and author of *Good Children*, says: "Smacking is the best way to deal with a young child who doesn't understand argument. It's much less harmful than using emotional punishment which can easily escalate and damage a child.

"Spoilt children are dreadful and if you don't smack your child when he's naughty he's likely to be spoilt because you are teaching him he can get away with things.

"It's completely wrong for so-called experts to say they know better than parents. And the problems if this law were passed would be truly horrifying."

Here, TESSA CUNNINGHAM talks to mothers with opposing views.

YES Violence solves nothing

Nurse Alice Cook has vowed never to raise a hand to her three-year-old son Jay – but she says that doesn't mean she's soft on discipline.

Alice, 39, who lives with husband Mick in London, says: "I would say I'm pretty firm with Jay. I set definite limits on what he can and can't do. He knows when I say no I mean it and I'm not going to give in even if he whines.

"It's much better to reward good behaviour and to teach by example. There are some things I insist on like bedtimes and brushing his teeth and I will not tolerate him hurting other children or drawing on the walls.

"But if he disobeys I don't punish him. I remove him from the situation and explain to him why I think he has behaved badly. For example he used to smack the cat. It never crossed my mind to smack him back.

"Instead whenever he did it I gave the cat a big cuddle. That showed Jay he wasn't going to get any attention by behaving naughtily and after a couple of weeks he stopped doing it.

"I try to keep one step ahead. I've made my home as childproof as I can and don't run round making sure he doesn't break things.

"The child will remember being smacked but not why.

"You may start off with a light slap but if the child keeps doing the same thing the thump will get harder. I definitely believe smacking should be banned.

"Of course he makes me furious but it's wrong to take out your frustrations on your child by hitting him. Instead I leave the room to cool off."

NO It helps kids to behave

Claire Elford was a nanny for seven years before starting her own family. Her job convinced her that naughty children who are never smacked can end up spoilt. Claire, 27, lives in London with husband Craig and children Amelia, three, and 18-month-old Archie.

She says, "The parents I worked for were often very soft on discipline and didn't believe in smacking so the kids got away with murder.

"They would whine until they got what they wanted by wearing their mums down. Many of them ended up spoilt because they knew they could get away with things.

"I vowed that was not going to happen with my children. I love them and I want them to grow up to be nice likeable people – not little monsters who think they can always have their own way.

"I definitely believe that light smacks are a very good way to discipline small children.

"They are too young to be reasoned with and simply get angry and frustrated if you sit them down and give them a long lecture on rights and wrongs. When Amelia is naughty I warn her not to carry on and if she persists I give her a light smack on the hand. She may cry but then she comes for a cuddle and we make up.

"Smacking defuses a situation. It's much more scary for a child to see her mum losing her temper than for the child to have a quick smack before the situation gets out of hand.

"But certainly by the times she's 10 I wouldn't expect to be smacking her."

© The Sun

16 International companies

On this and the following pages, you can read about how business has become truly global. When British people telephone their bank or insurance company, the conversation is, of course, conducted in English and any transactions are done by computer. So the caller has no idea if the operator is just around the corner or on the other side of the world. In fact, the call is often answered by an operator 7,000 kilometres away in India. Indian call centres are now big business and they deal with millions of calls a week from the UK. What happens, however, when a British customer wants to talk to the operator about a favourite soap opera or the weather in the UK, if the operator has never been to the UK? To solve this problem, Indian call centres run classes in 'the British way of life'.

1 Before you read, discuss the following.

What image do you have of Britain in general? Why do you feel this way?

Imagine you go to one of 'the British way of life' classes. What else would you expect to learn about 'being British'?

Glossary

1. BT: British Telecom, one of the UK's main telephone companies.
2. pukka: originally an Indian word which means genuine, perfect or really good.
3. EastEnders, Emmerdale and Coronation Street: popular television soap operas.
4. Yes Minister: a long-running television comedy series about politics.

2 As you read, answer the questions to find the meaning of these words.

a Does *the chances are* mean possibly or probably?
b Does *a string of* mean some or many?
c Does *shifting* mean moving or reducing?
d Does *drizzle* mean light rain or bright sunshine?
e Does *put through to* mean connected to or ignored by?
f Does *impeccable* mean quite good or absolutely perfect?
g Does *steeped in* mean without or filled with?
h Does *lilting* mean flat and boring or rising and falling?
i Does *rigorous* mean easy or difficult?
j Does *took on* mean hired or fired?
k Is a *troubleshooter* a person who makes trouble or someone who solves problems?
l Does *booming* mean growing fast or getting worse?

3 Now complete these sentences with words or information from the article.

a British Telecom has transferred its _____ service to India.

b Computer clocks are adjusted because India is _____ hours behind UK time.

c Operators learn about traditional British dishes such as _____ and _____ pie.

d Starting salaries of around £ _____ a year are about 20% of UK rates.

e The call centre operators are _____ educated, often having a university degree.

f Staff watch videos of popular _____ operas like Coronation Street.

g Operators use _____ instead of their real names.

h Business is booming and Whipro Spectramind took on 6,600 new _____ last month at its four _____ in Delhi, Mumbai, Chennai and Pune.

i Most of the staff are young and _____ .

j Small talk with English customers is mainly about the _____ and their _____ .

HOW THE INDIAN CALL CENTRE MAKES YOU FEEL AT HOME

Hangin' on the Delhi phone

When you pick up the phone to chat to a British company, the chances are your call will go to INDIA.

For more and more companies are saving cash by basing their call centres in the distant sub-continent.

This week it was announced that BT are planning to move their directory enquiries service to operators based in India. They are just the latest in a string of firms shifting operations abroad – and the chances are callers will not notice the difference.

Because the latest call centres in Delhi are as British as any office here – with pukka English accents and staff kept up to date with the UK weather, EastEnders and Coronation Street so they can make conversation over the phone.

The Sun went to Delhi to visit the country's third biggest call centre, Whipro Spectramind, to see how locals learn the British way of life.

The temperature outside was well over 80F when I visited. But the employees had checked the BBC's online weather map and as they talked to customers the chat was all about drizzle in the UK.

In the corner of their screens the clocks were set to British time – five and a half hours behind. In many booths where the operators work, walls are covered with photos of UK sportsmen and film stars. Workers keep up with the news on the other side of the world by reading the BBC's website and, of course, The Sun Online at the start of the day.

The call operators are as comfortable talking about steak and kidney pies as they are about English actors.

Call centres are huge business in India – where workers' salaries start at around £2,000 per year.

Where once your query about insurance or your credit card balance was put through to a centre in Cardiff or Newcastle, today your telephone call is rerouted 4,400 miles.

As well as being cheap to employ, the Indian worker is keen and well educated. The vast majority of trainees are graduates and their English is impeccable.

But the key to success of the Indian companies is attention to detail. All Whipro Spectramind trainees are steeped in British culture and even undergo voice training to make them sound less Indian. The company's Raja Varadarajan says: "We want our staff to empathise with the people they are speaking to. So cultural awareness is very important. We show them videos of soap operas, films and sport. Yes Minister is a favourite as is Coronation Street and Emmerdale. We are not trying to pretend we are British. We are making sure we can interact."

Just as much emphasis is put on the need for the trainees to lose their lilting Indian accents.

Whipro Spectramind also runs call centres for American firms and help with the training of other workers to deal with callers from the US.

Whipro Spectramind is open 24 hours, seven days a week. Walking around the huge offices you hear local English accents so good you could be in Oxford. In other areas you hear convincing American tones.

Apart from the accents and knowledgeable small talk, most call operators are trained to avoid revealing where they are based.

Raja denies that his company is being deceptive. He says: "Some customers are happy for us to chat about where we are. But others prefer us to avoid the issue because there is no need." The call operators also use aliases, so instead of being greeted by Sanjeeta or Raj, you will find yourself chatting to Sarah or Rob. By taking Western names the callers also feel like they are on familiar ground.

Despite the rigorous training process, many Indians would love to work in a call centre.

Doubles

If the company places an advert in the Hindustan Times newspaper they expect thousands of applications.

But for every 100 applicants only seven or eight go through the training. Whipro Spectramind already has 6,600 employees in its four branches in Delhi, Mumbai, Chennai and Pune.

Last month, Whipro Spectramind took on 800 new employees. Experts estimate that the Indian call centre industry doubles in size every month.

Deepak Nigam, 26, is a science graduate and learning to be a troubleshooter on a technical desk. He has been training for two weeks and already decided on an alias – Daryl.

Deepak says: "This is a very good job because call centres are booming. It is the right place to be. I am very happy to have this job."

The vast majority of employees in the immaculate air-conditioned offices are young and trendy.

As well as those wearing traditional Indian clothing, many of them are in Levi jeans and Nike trainers and all are keen to embrace the culture of a country that many of them will never see.

And such an attitude is good for our business. Papiya Sakar, the Delhi training manager, says: "We talk to English people mainly about the weather and their pets. Pretty much every caller mentions the weather – there is no escaping it."

© The Sun

Now read about some brands that are known all over the world.

NEWSPAPER ARTICLES TO GET TEENAGERS TALKING — Work and education

Coca Cola, Nike and Toyota are now known all over the world. But where do their brand names originally come from?

4) Before you read, discuss the following.
Look at the 17 brand names mentioned in the article. How many of them do you recognise? What are these companies famous for?

Glossary

1 ain't (colloquial): isn't
2 grand: great, really good. *Ain't life brand* is a pun on the phrase *ain't life grand* (=life is good)
3 delves into: investigates, finds out about
4 Aston Martin: a make of sports car
5 Tesco: a British supermarket chain
6 first mate: an officer on a ship

5) As you read, answer these questions. Which brand name (or names):

a comes from Greek mythology?

b comes from a famous novel?

c is connected with a particular place name?

d was not the first choice of the founder?

e takes its name from a number and a nut?

f sounds like an enormous number?

g comes from the names of a leaf and a nut?

h suggests that the product has medical qualities?

i comes from someone's nickname?

j combines the names of two people and has its origins in tea?

k is named after a type of spider?

l comes from a Scandinavian language?

6) Now discuss the following.

a Many big companies set up factories or call centres abroad. What do you think of these companies? Are they helping local people? Or do they do it for other reasons?
b What is *globalisation* and how is it changing the world?
c Do you think that the internet and the phone bring people together? Or do you think they make people look, sound and think the same?
d Will the time come when we all wear the same clothes, watch the same TV programmes, eat the same food and live in the same way? Or will we become more individual in a world full of choices?

7) Imagine Indian call centre operators are being taught about your country. What ten things would they need to learn about your way of life?

Further information
The two websites mentioned in the article are *www.bbc.co.uk* and *www.thesun.co.uk*.

STORIES BEHIND THE NAMES YOU KNOW

AIN'T LIFE BRAND

They are the brand names that have become part of everyday life. Here, CAROLINE IGGULDEN delves into a new book to reveal how some of our most famous firms got their names.

ADIDAS
The German sports goods firm is named after founder Adolf, nickname Adi Dassler.

ASTON MARTIN
The Aston Hill races near Birmingham where the firm was founded provided the inspiration for the first part of the name. The second is named after founder Lionel Martin.

COCA-COLA
Derived from the coca leaves and kola nuts that were part of the original flavouring of the drink.

EBAY
Pierre Omidyar, founder of the online auction site, wanted to use the name of his internet consultancy Echo Bay Technology Group. But Echo Bay Mines had already registered a similar name so he called it eBay instead.

GOOGLE
The name is taken from the word googol – a vast number represented by 1 followed by 100 noughts. It started as a boast about the amount of information the online search engine would cover.

HARIBO
The German confectioner derives its name from the first letters of its founder, Hans Riegel, and Bonn, the firm's home city.

IKEA
The Swedish furniture maker was founded by Ingvar Kamprad whose family home was a farm called Elmtaryd near the Swedish village of Agunnaryd, giving the store the initials IKEA.

LEGO
From a Danish phrase, leg godt, which means "play well".

LYCOS
This search engine's name was inspired by the family name of wolf spiders who are excellent hunters.

MITSUBISHI
The Japanese car manufacturer's name refers to its three-diamond logo. It is a combination of the words "mitsu", meaning three and "hishi", meaning water chestnut, a word denoting a diamond shape in Japanese.

NIKE
The US sports firm is named after the Greek goddess of victory.

NOKIA
Named after a small town in Finland that was home to a successful pulp and paper company that expanded into rubber goods. It later hit on the idea of producing mobile phones.

PEPSI
Originally called Brad's Drink, it was a concoction formulated by pharmacist Caleb Bradham. In 1898, it was renamed Pepsi cola after the kola nuts and pepsin – an enzyme produced in the stomach that helps digestion.

STARBUCKS
Named after Starbuck, the first mate in the novel Moby Dick.

TESCO
Founder Sir Jack Cohen started selling groceries in London's East End in 1919. Tesco's name first appeared on tea packets in 1924. It was based on TE Stockwell, a partner in the firm of tea suppliers and the first two letters of Cohen.

TOYOTA
Sakichi Toyoda called his company Toyeda, but changed it after running a competition to find a new one. Toyota is written with eight strokes in Japanese script – a lucky number in the country.

YAHOO!
The name is an acronym for "Yet Another Hierarchical Officious Oracle", but the company's founders also liked the definition of yahoo as "rude, unsophisticated, uncouth" taken from the book Gulliver's Travels.

© The Economist Business Miscellany

NEWSPAPER ARTICLES TO GET TEENAGERS TALKING — Work and education

17 From teacher to plumber

The articles on pages 50 and 51 appeared on the same day in two different papers, *The Sun* (a popular tabloid) and *The Daily Telegraph* (a more serious broadsheet). They are about a university professor called Dr Karl Gensberg, who was unhappy about his pay. One day, a plumber came to install a boiler in Dr Gensberg's house and the two men got talking about how much money they earned.

1 Before you read, discuss the following.
What do you think happened next?
Do you think the newspapers will cover the story in the same way?

2 As you read, complete the crossword with twelve words from the two articles.

Across
2 Dr Gensberg has quit his job and other teachers may follow …
3 talking (in a relaxed, informal way)
4 installing (boilers)
5 absolutely amazed, astonished (slang)
9 brilliant scientist (slang)
11 this produces hot water to heat a house
13 incredible

Glossary

The Sun
1 skint (slang): penniless
2 boffin (slang): a brilliant scientist
3 brainbox (slang): very clever
4 a Phd: a Doctor of Philosophy, the highest university qualification
5 gobsmacked (slang): astonished, very surprised
6 plum (informal): fantastic, wonderful

Daily Telegraph
1 only to realise: but then realised
2 follow suit: do the same
3 in their droves: in large numbers

Down
1 leaving, abandoning, resigning from
6 penniless (slang)
7 x 2
8 monthly pay
10 very intelligent (slang)
12 a detailed study of a subject, to understand it better

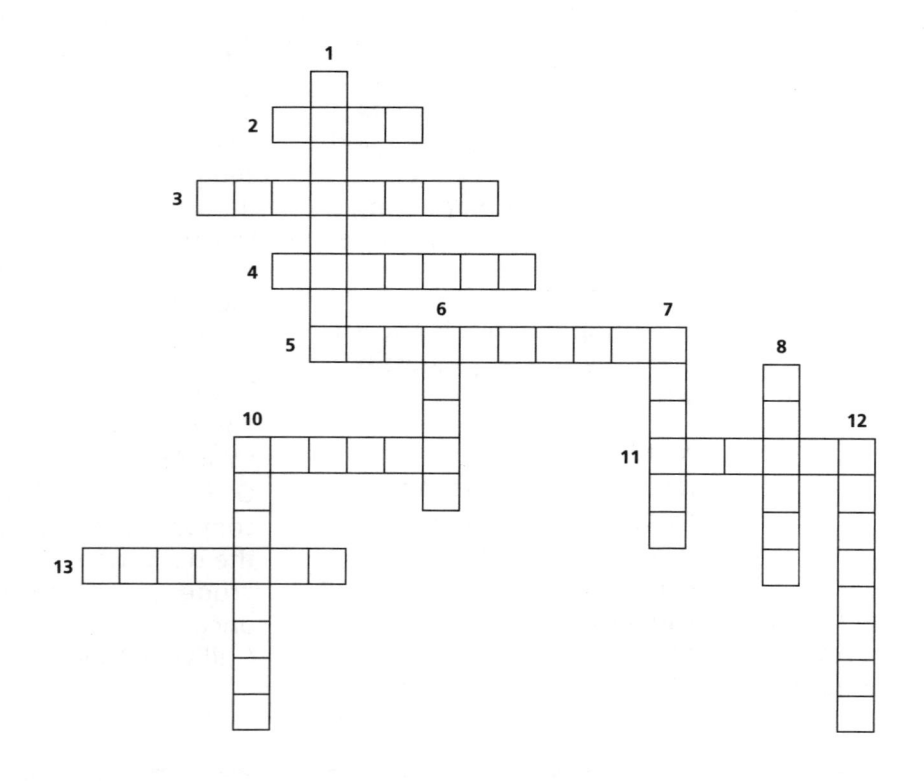

NEWSPAPER ARTICLES TO GET TEENAGERS TALKING Work and education

3) Now complete these sentences with words or information from the articles.

a Dr Gensberg earned £ _____ a year as a molecular biologist, about £ _____ less than his plumber.

b University lecturers are going on _____ for a week to protest about their pay.

c One of Dr Gensberg's colleagues now runs a _____ in France.

d Another is thinking about _____ the Royal Mail.

e The plumber came to install a _____ in Dr Gensberg's house.

f The plumber was _____ when he saw the doctor's pay slip.

g Dr Gensberg's university _____ ends in April.

h It is very sad that so many people like Mr Gensberg are leaving higher _____ .

i Plumbing is now such a popular career that it is hard to find a _____ to enrol on.

j The Institute of Plumbing says that some plumbers are earning _____ £50,000 a year.

'Our plumber used to be a molecular biologist'

4) Now discuss the following.

Use this useful language.
- *The teacher would be better off as a plumber.* (= better paid, in a better situation)
- *It's difficult to make ends meet on his salary.* (= he finds it difficult to pay all his bills)
- *I get peanuts.* (= my pay is really bad)
- *If you pay peanuts, you get monkeys.*
- *a well-paid/a badly-paid job*
- *a skilled worker/a highly skilled worker*
- *a workaholic* (= someone who works too much; compare: an *alcoholic*, *shopoholic*)
- *to work like a dog* (= to work really hard)
- *a blue-collar worker* (= someone who does manual work, ie works with their hands, like a plumber)
- *a white-collar worker* (= someone who does non-manual work, like a teacher)
- *your take home pay* (= the money you receive after tax has been deducted)

a Who should get more money, a plumber or a teacher? Why?

b Why are most footballers better paid than a nurse?

c Which of these people are paid:
a) too much? b) too little? c) about the right amount?

pop stars	surgeons	police officers
waiters	television presenters	cleaners
actors	builders	shop assistants

d What do you think is the most important thing about a job: the pay, the people you work with or the job satisfaction?

e How important is work? Do you want to 'work to live' or 'live to work'?

5) With your group, discuss the main differences between the articles in *The Sun* and *The Daily Telegraph*. Think about the following.

a What kind of language do they use (slang, formal, informal etc.)?

b Is there a difference in the use of headlines and photographs?

c Which of the two papers is easier to read?

d Which gives the most information?

Now in your groups, talk about a story in the news. Plan a paragraph in the style of *The Sun* and one in the style of the *Daily Telegraph*. Present your stories to the class.

SKINT BOFFIN QUITS TO BE RICH PLUMBER

Top scientist will double his £23,000 salary

By John Scott

A BRAINBOX scientist is quitting his job – to double his pay as a PLUMBER.

Dr Karl Gensberg, a molecular biologist, decided on the career change after realising how little he earned compared to skilled and in-demand tradesmen.

He hopes to make twice as much as the £23,000 salary he was on at Birmingham University following a 13-year career in academic research.

News of the amazing job switch came as thousands of university lecturers started a week-long series of strikes over pay yesterday.

Dr Gensberg, 41, told how he decided to make the change after chatting to a plumber who was fitting a boiler in his home.

The dad of one from Streetly, West Midlands, said: "He assumed I had loads of money as I had a PhD. I showed him my pay slip and he was gobsmacked. He said he earned £33,000 and some colleagues took home £50,000.

"I just thought, 'What am I doing? My work is a combination of zero career structure, contractual abuse and pathetic pay.' I love molecular biology, but I'm looking forward to a better way of life.'"

He is training as a plumber two days a week at Sutton Coldfield College and goes full time in July.

A university spokeswoman said his contract was due to end soon and he had been given "time off and flexibility in his working hours to pursue another career".

The Institute of Plumbing said reports of salaries of up to £120,000 a year were exaggerated, although there is a huge skills shortage in the industry.

© The Sun

Biologist abandons vital research to double his salary fitting boilers

By Sally Pook

A MOLECULAR biologist whose research could help arthritis and cancer sufferers is to abandon his academic career for a better paid job as a gas fitter.

Karl Gensberg, 41, has been a postdoctoral research fellow at the University of Birmingham for 13 years but says he can no longer afford to work on short-term contracts in the education sector.

The scientist, who is married with a son, spent six years studying human biology and molecular microbiology only to realise he could earn more money and have more job security fitting boilers.

Mr Gensberg, who earns £23,000, believes that unless conditions in the profession improve, more academics will be forced to follow suit.

He knows of two other colleagues who have left Birmingham, one to run a boarding house in France. The other is considering joining the Royal Mail.

"My plumber was fitting my boiler and said he assumed I had loads of money because I had a Phd," Mr Gensburg said. "I happened to have my pay slip to hand and showed it to him and he was abusolutely gobsmacked. He said he earned £33,000 and some of his colleagues took home £50,000. I just thought, what am I doing? My work is a combination of zero career structure, contractual abuse and pathetic pay, which is a pretty poor package."

Mr Gensberg, of Streetly, Walsall, studied for his degree and PhD at Aston University and then started work at Birmingham, where he has been on four short-term contracts. Each time a contract comes to an end, he has to compete for another, sometimes at a lower salary than he was previously earning. On one occasion, he took a £5,000 pay cut.

"I feel like a fool," he said. "My plumber probably left school at 16 and has probably always earned more than me. I am just not prepared to keep looking around for jobs that are so badly paid. The university has never offered me a staff job. It is incredibly frustrating and I feel my education was a complete waste of taxpayers' money."

Mr Gensberg has been carrying out research into the effects of electro-magnetic fields on the body. He believes his work, which investigates how wounds heal, could eventually help to relieve the pain of arthritis sufferers and cancer patients.

He says no one has so far made proper molecular studies into how such fields can speed up the healing of wounds on the body.

Mr Gensberg is now studying part time at Sutton Coldfield college in Birmingham and will qualify as a fulltime gas fitter in July. He completes his contract at the university in April.

"I know it is extreme but I can't see any other way. I always thought if I worked hard I would progress, but it doesn't seem to work that way."

Mr Gensberg is not alone in feeling badly paid. Thousands of academic staff began a week long series of strikes yesterday after they rejected a three per cent pay offer. More than 1,200 staff at Birmingham are expected to strike.

The Association of University Teachers (AUT) says academics' pay has fallen behind other employees by up to 40 per cent in the last 20 years.

At least 2,000 staff are leaving Britain for America and Europe, where they can earn up to 50 per cent more, according to the AUT's figures.

"The tragedy is that there are hundreds of people like Mr Gensberg who are doing work of national or international importance who are now leaving higher education in Britain in their droves," said Paul Rees, a spokesman for the AUT.

Mr Gensberg claimed that when he told the university of his plans, they said they might offer him a job as a gas fitter.

A spokesman for the university could not confirm this. In a statement, it said: "Dr Karl Gensberg is employed on a fixed-term contract which will end shortly and therefore the university has been seeking to redeploy him.

"He has been given time off and flexibility in his working hours to pursue another career."

The Institute of Plumbing said it was difficult to enrol on gas-fitting and plumbing courses because so many people believe it is well-paid. A spokesman said: "The average salary is about £30,000 but you can earn up to £50,000."

© The Daily Telegraph

NEWSPAPER ARTICLES TO GET TEENAGERS TALKING — Work and education

18 Does punctuation matter?

Languages like French and Arabic are regulated by famous academies. These can tell you the correct rules of grammar and the right way to spell words. English, however, has no official rules for grammar, spelling or punctuation. As a result, many British children never study grammar at school and you do not lose marks in most UK exams if you make a mistake in spelling or grammar.

1 Before you read, discuss the following.

a Would you lose marks in your exams if you made such mistakes?
b Do we need punctuation in an age of text messaging and e-mails? If we do need these rules, who should decide what is right and wrong?
c The market trader in the article is from the East End of London and speaks a famous dialect of English called *cockney*. Cockneys often drop the first or last letter of a word so *here* is pronounced '*ere* and *of* becomes a short *o*'. What do you think the cockney sentence '*As 'e go' a big 'ouse?* means?

Glossary

1 to yearn for something (a literary word): to want something very much
2 let me be: leave me alone

Never mind the punctuation, look at our low price's

The misplaced apostrophe is a sign of the times but there are few complaints in the East End, writes **Pav Akhtar**

"ERE, have a pound o' these," said Alan Old, a greengrocer more concerned with selling things than grammar, in a charming attempt to sell me some marrows I did not need.

"People round here don't care much for spelling and the like. All they're interested in is getting the price. The best price."

Misuse of the apostrophe is so commonplace, according to research by the Oxford Dictionary of English, that it may become "acceptable".

Mr Old, 49, was standing behind rows of green beans at his stall on the Roman Road Market, east London. His goods were advertised on signs littered with misused apostrophes.

"So what if I've spelt something incorrectly? No one notices. Just as long as the carrots are carrots and corn is corn, they're happy."

Danny Wilson, 16, from Dagenham, east London agreed: "Grammar is not that important. Nobody really takes any notice. For example, when you are sending a text message on your phone, you just abbreviate everything and, when you're doing that, the rules for spelling go out of the window and grammar is not even a consideration."

Not all shoppers in the market were so indifferent. Caroline Willson, 24, from Hornchurch, east London, is about to start a teacher training course at Canterbury Christ Church University College.

"It is very important that you are able to write a sentence properly. If you can't, it reflects badly on you. It's a shame that people have little idea of how to use English grammar properly."

Her mother, Gill, 48, offered parental support. "I come from the traditionalist viewpoint that punctuation and grammar are important to our day-to-day lives. It's relevant because it helps us to speak our language properly. It worries me that so many children do not know how to write using the correct grammar."

Tony Hassan, 41, a clothing trader from north London, was unapologetic about several improper uses of the apostrophe on his stall.

"Does a customer want to know about the price, or does she want to know whether I've spelt 'its' in the grammatically correct way?"

Petra Hayes, 30, from Hackney, east London, a fellow stall-holder, disagreed. "Even if it's lingerie, like my stall, you won't find a word misspelt or a point of grammar overlooked."

There was indeed nothing – grammatically – at fault on her stall.

Paul Oakley, 35, a greengrocer on the market, is also a staunch defender of correct grammar usage. "It makes a good impression if people can see you have spelt things correctly, and have the grammar right. If you make mistakes, people notice and some of them even point it out. I take the time to write things out properly."

Paul Dashford, 37, a fellow greengrocer, was more acerbic. "People around here don't even know what an apostrophe is. So what do they care?"

Brenda Humphries, 55, from Camden, north London, has been teaching English for 30 years. "Grammar is extremely important," she insisted. "Too many children now depend on the spell and grammar check facility computers offer. It's a losing battle, I'm afraid."

© The Daily Telegraph

NEWSPAPER ARTICLES TO GET TEENAGERS TALKING — Work and education

2 As you read, complete the crossword with words from the text to reveal the name of a common punctuation mark.

1 She sells vegetables from a _____ in the market.
2 When texting, you _____ words to make them shorter.
3 A _____ is a green vegetable often eaten with rice or meat.
4 When texting, rules of spelling go out of the _____ .
5 The Oxford Dictionary of English carried out some _____ into how British people use the apostrophe.
6 A _____ is about half a kilo.
7 You'll have to type this letter again. It's _____ with mistakes.
8 If Paul Oakley misuses the apostrophe on his signs, some of his customers will _____ out the mistake.
9 The misuse of the apostrophe has become _____ in recent years.

3 Now match A and B to make sentences about the article.

A
1 Alan Old and Tony Hassan say their customers ...
2 Danny Wilson says grammar ...
3 Caroline Willson suggests that ...
4 Gill Wilson is worried that ...
5 Paul Oakley takes the time to ...
6 Brenda Humphreys points out that children ...

B
a ... now rely on computer programs to correct their spelling.
b ... get all his signs right.
c ... are more interested in prices than correct grammar.
d ... you make a bad impression if your grammar is poor.
e ... is irrelevant when you send a text message.
f ... too many children never learn correct grammar.

4 Now discuss the following.

a Which of the speakers do you agree with?
b Is it important to know the rules of spelling and punctuation when you speak a language? Or is Danny Wilson right when he says, *Grammar is not that important. Nobody really takes any notice*?
c How well do you know the grammar of your mother tongue?
d Do you judge people by the way they use grammar?
e Do you think English should have an academy to lay down rules for what is right and wrong? Or do you like the idea that a language can be anything you want it to be?

5 Read the letters below. Explain how the punctuation changes the meaning.

Dear Jack,
I want a man who knows what love is all about. You are generous, kind, thoughtful. People who are not like you admit to being useless and inferior. You have ruined me for other men. I yearn for you. I have no feelings whatsoever when we are apart. I can be forever happy - will you let me be yours?
Jill

Dear Jack,
I want a man who knows what love is. All about you are generous, kind, thoughtful people, who are not like you. Admit to being useless and inferior. You have ruined me. For other men, I yearn. For you, I have no feelings whatsoever. When we're apart, I can be forever happy. Will you let me be?
Yours, Jill

6 Can you punctuate these sentences in more than one way? How does it change the meaning? Compare your answers with a friend.

a David thought Caroline looked really tired.
  David thought Caroline looked really tired.

b A woman without her man is nothing.
  A woman without her man is nothing.

c The girls who had finished the exam left the room.
  The girls who had finished the exam left the room.

Work and education

19 Does prison work?

For Luigi Pagano, the Governor of the San Vittore jail in Milan, a prison is not just a place where you punish criminals for their crimes. He believes that prisoners should work a full day, learning new job skills that they can take with them when they go back into society. In his attempts to rehabilitate prisoners in this way, Mr Pagano has come up with an unusual idea.

1 Before you read, discuss the following.

Should prisoners work seven hours a day like other people?
Should they be paid for that work?
What sorts of jobs could they do?

Glossary

1 crooks: criminals
2 directory inquiries: a call centre service that provides phone numbers
3 daylight robbery: obviously overcharging
4 Telecom Italia: a major Italian telephone company
5 a pilot scheme: a trial, an experimental scheme
6 purpose-built: specially designed
7 the takings: the amount of money you earn from selling goods or services
8 inmates: prisoners
9 Mafiosi: members of the Mafia

Italian crooks are helping with inquiries

Hilary Clarke, Rome

SOME of Britain's new directory enquiry services may be accused of daylight robbery, but only in Italy are there operators who will openly admit to being a bunch of crooks.

Telecom Italia confirmed last week that callers to directory inquiries may find themselves talking to murderers and armed robbers.

Under a pilot scheme believed to be the first of its kind in Europe, inmates at the San Vittore jail in Milan are being paid up to £700 a month to man a purpose-built call centre in a prison wing.

In seven-hour shifts the prisoners give not only telephone numbers, but also the share prices, cinema and theatre listings and advice on restaurants – the food, not the time of night the takings are counted.

Callers are not told that the people on the other end of the line are in jail; nor are the operators allowed to divulge this.

"A new frontier has opened in prison labour," said Luigi Pagano, the director of San Vittore. It reflected prison philosophy that inmates should not regard captivity as "an excuse to remain inert", he added.

Thirty prisoners have been recruited to the scheme, which started last month. They underwent a rigorous three-week training course. This included learning how to deal with the public, perhaps in a less confrontational style than hitherto.

The participants include murderers, armed robbers and drug dealers. Mafiosi and child abusers, however, are call-barred.

Marco Tronchettie Provera, chairman of Telecom Italia, said the inmates' contracts were identical to those of 2,000 other operators at 73 conventional call centres around the country.

"The point is that this is a real job," he said.

Prisoners have welcomed the project, which helps their families financially and gives them contact with the outside world.

"This is an unprecedented opportunity for us," said an inmate named only as Massimo, 25, who is serving four years for arms and drug offences. "We get the feeling of doing the same job as people on the outside."

Telecom Itialia is hoping to extend its startling recruitment policy to other jails in the future.

© The Sunday Times

NEWSPAPER ARTICLES TO GET TEENAGERS TALKING   Work and education

2 **As you read, match the words from the article 1–10 with their meanings a–j.**

1 bunch	a)	prisoners
2 a pilot scheme	b)	new, happening for the first time
3 inmates	c)	periods of work
4 shifts	d)	forbidden, banned
5 divulge	e)	testing something out
6 captivity	f)	reveal (the truth, a secret)
7 inert	g)	group, gang
8 rigorous	h)	inactive, doing nothing
9 barred	i)	imprisonment, life behind bars
10 unprecedented	j)	hard, tough, difficult

3 **Now circle T (True) or F (False).**

a Murderers and armed robbers are taking part in the project.   T / F
b There are several similar schemes across Europe.   T / F
c The inmates are not paid for the work they do.   T / F
d The prisoners work a nine-hour shift.   T / F
e The service also provides information about cinemas and restaurants.   T / F
f Inmates must tell callers they are speaking from a jail.   T / F
g The three-week training course is not that difficult.   T / F
h Some categories of prisoners are banned from the scheme.   T / F
i Thanks to the scheme, prisoners can send money to their families   T / F
j Telecom Italia wants to set up similar projects in other jails   T / F

4 **Now discuss the following.**

1 Why do we send people to prison?
2 Should we use prison to punish people or to rehabilitate them?
3 Do prisoners have human rights? Or do you lose your human rights when you commit a crime?
4 What sorts of people should not be sent to prison? What about pregnant women, young teenagers or people with mental problems?

5 **Look at the 'crimes' below. In groups, decide on the best punishment for each crime. Use the useful language and the punishments in the box.**

a fine	community service	imprisonment
	the death penalty/execution	acquitted

a dropping litter on the street
b using a mobile phone while driving a car
c not paying your fare on a bus or train
d shoplifting
e mugging an old lady
f joyriding (stealing a car, driving it for a while and then abandoning it)
g drink driving
h taking drugs
i manslaughter
j premeditated murder
k war crimes
l acts of terrorism

Use this useful language.
• to be charged with (a crime)
• to be convicted of (a crime)
• to be found guilty/not guilty of (a crime)
• to be given (100 hours) community service
• to be fined (£1,000)
• to be sentenced to (three years in jail)
• to be given a (three-year) sentence for …
• to be imprisoned/sent to prison for (three years)
• to be released from prison after (three years)
• to rehabilitate a person: to help a person to return to society
• to be acquitted: to be freed, to be found not guilty

6 **In groups, think of a recent crime that people are talking about on TV or in the papers, or imagine one of the crimes in exercise 5 above. Write detailed notes about what happened and who was involved.**

a Decide what the punishment should be or should have been.
b Present the case to the rest of the class.

We've chosen the case of _____ . He/She was charged with _____ .

What happened was that he/she _____ . The victim was _____ .

We've decided he/she should be/should have been found guilty/not guilty of _____ because _____ .

His/her punishment should be …

Do the other groups agree or disagree with the punishment you have chosen?

20 The island doctor

A new life on Jura is just what the doctor ordered

Island finds a GP with help from the Telegraph, reports **Auslan Cramb**

THE scenery is breathtaking, the neighbourhood is crime-free, the whisky is exceptional and the school has just 16 pupils.

But the Isle of Jura has just spent a year without a doctor because – the residents were told – no one wanted to earn £100,000 a year as a GP on one of Britain's most beautiful islands.

Last autumn the islanders insisted on taking over the task of finding a new doctor and suggested a "one month on, one month off" system with two people sharing the post.

They were convinced nobody had applied because the health board's "tiny" advert in the *British Medical Journal* failed to explain the attractions of island life.

They were proved correct within days of the story appearing in *The Daily Telegraph*, when they were inundated with applications.

Doctors from all over Europe, including some from Italy and Spain, contacted the island in the hope of escaping stressful urban surgeries.

One of the 36 applicants was Dr Murray Grigor, 37, who visited Jura in December with this wife Janet, 37, and their daughter Rachel, four.

"It was an absolutely beautiful day," he said. "The sun was shining and when we saw the scenery we knew it was right for us."

He was initially interested in job-sharing, but applied for a full-time position after the family "fell in love" with the place as soon as they stepped off the ferry from the neighbouring island of Islay.

The job comes with a bungalow and surgery overlooking the sea, and the primary school is next door.

Dr Grigor was offered the post in January and this week found himself in unfamiliar territory as a country GP with more than enough time for his patients. He has swapped 1,500 patients at a busy practice in Livingston, a suburb of Edinburgh, for 175 on Jura.

In the busiest surgeries in England, a single doctor may have 3,000 patients to care for.

He will be on call around the clock, but will be compensated with a payment of around £40,000 for out-of-hours cover on top of his salary of £60,000.

With such a small population, the new GP does not expect regular evening calls. "We both enjoyed Livingston," said Dr Grigor. "But we wanted to bring up Rachel in a rural setting.

"Jura is a beautiful island, a safe place for children and we have found the community very friendly."

'This is a happy ending to what seemed like a real crisis for the island'

"When Rachel goes into primary one after the summer she will be in a class of three. At her last school there were 60 in her year."

He had previously worked as a "locum" doctor in the Highlands, and also in Tower Hamlets and Clapham in London. His new post could not offer a bigger contrast to an inner-city practice.

The main link with the outside world is the ferry from Islay, which has eight malt whisky distilleries.

Jura, which is 29 miles long and mostly deserted, has its own Isle of Jura distillery behind the only hotel in the island's only village, and also a general store and a tea room.

It is famed for its deer stalking, salmon fishing and white sand beaches and is instantly identifiable because of its distinctive mountains, the 2,600ft-high Paps of Jura.

Dr Grigor is learning the bagpipes, his wife plays the clarsach and is a Gaelic primary teacher, and the couple hope to develop their interest in traditional music.

"On our first visit to Jura we both thought, 'What a difference from Clapham,'" he added.

"We had promised ourselves that one day we would come back to the Highlands, but we weren't looking for a job until my aunt called after reading the paper and told me, 'I have found the perfect job for you'. I think a doctor in a rural area like this has the role of an old-fashioned family doctor, and that is the way I like to work." Dr Grigor plans to look for another GP to work a long weekend once a month to give him a break from 24-hour cover, and to allow the family to visit relatives in Edinburgh and Fife. He will also operate the island's first ambulance, a second-hand vehicle bought by Alisdair Cooper, a Scottish businessman based in Halifax whose grandparents once ran the island shop. A regular visitor to Jura, he said he had donated the refurbished ambulance this week to "give back something to a special community".

Gwen Boardman, 61, one of the residents involved in finding the new doctor, said the islanders were delighted to have a GP again. "We were told no one was interested in coming to such a beautiful place. But the health board had just placed a tiny advert in the BMJ. As soon as the story appeared in the *Telegraph*, the response was amazing. Now we have a new doctor, another pupil in the school, our own ambulance and a happy ending to what seemed last year like a real crisis on the island."

© The Daily Telegraph

NEWSPAPER ARTICLES TO GET TEENAGERS TALKING — Work and education

The island of Jura lies four kilometres off the west coast of Scotland. It is home to wild goats, seals, golden eagles and over a hundred species of birds. It is 42 kilometres long and 11 kilometres wide, but most of the island is wild and uninhabited and only 175 people live there. The island has just one road, one shop, one school and one hotel. In 2005, the inhabitants of Jura advertised for a doctor to come and live on the island.

1 Before you read, discuss the following.

What kind of response do you think the islanders got? Would you want to live and work somewhere like this?

Glossary

1 just what the doctor ordered: just what you need
2 a GP (General Practitioner): a family doctor
3 board: committee
4 British Medical Journal (BMJ): a magazine for doctors
5 the set-up: the way things are organised
6 out-of-hours: not during the usual working day
7 locum: temporary replacement doctor
8 Tower Hamlets and Clapham: areas of London
9 inner-city: an often poor area in the centre of a big city
10 malt whisky distilleries: factories making whisky
11 clarsach and bagpipes: Scottish musical instruments
12 Gaelic: a language spoken in the north of Scotland

2 As you read, match the words from the article 1–9 with their meanings a–i.

1 breathtaking
2 idyllic
3 surgery
4 bungalow
5 neighbouring
6 swapped
7 around the clock
8 deserted
9 refurbished

a) empty, abandoned
b) cleaned, painted and repaired
c) small, single-storey house
d) perfect
e) where a doctor works
f) spectacular, fabulous, incredible
g) very close, nearby
h) 24 hours a day
i) exchanged

3 Now complete these sentences with words or information from the article.

a There is _____ crime on the island of Jura and the local school has only _____ pupils.
b The islanders spent a _____ without a _____, but when an _____ appeared in *The Daily Telegraph*, they were _____ with applications from all over Europe.
c The Grigors now live in a _____ overlooking the _____ .
d Before he came to Jura, Dr Grigor looked after _____ patients in a busy surgery.
e His daughter used to have _____ other pupils in her year. Now she will have just _____ classmates.
f To get to Jura from the neighbouring island of Islay, you need to take a _____ .
g Jura is famous for its _____ stalking, _____ fishing, white _____ beaches and a distillery that produces _____ .
h The Grigors are learning to play traditional musical _____ like the clarsach and the bagpipes.
i It was Dr Grigor's _____ who first spotted the advert in the paper.
j Dr Grigor will drive the refurbished _____ donated by Alisdair Couper.

4 Now discuss the following questions.

a Could you live in a place like Jura? What would it be like?
b What would you miss if you lived there? What would you gain?
c Why do so many people leave the countryside to live in big towns and cities?
d Are city people different from country people?
e What matters to you most, your standard of living or your quality of life?

5 Two schools – the inner-city Tower Hamlets High School and the Jura Island School – want to recruit a new teacher and they have asked your class to help.

a Divide into two groups, one supporting the Tower Hamlets School and the other supporting the Jura Island School.
b Think of reasons why your school is the best place to work. Use the following language.

Group 1
Come to The Tower Hamlets High School. An inner-city is a great place to live and work because ...
Don't go to Jura because ...

Group 2
Come to the Jura Island School. Jura is a great place to live and work because ...
Don't go to an inner-city school because ...

Now try to persuade your teacher to take up the job at the school you support. Which school would your teacher prefer?

21 A man's job?

One of the great sights of Venice is the gondolas taking tourists down the canals of the city. But if you look carefully, you will notice that all the gondoliers are men. This article is about a German woman called Alexandra Hai who wanted to become the first female gondolier in history.

1 Before you read, discuss the following.
What do you think happened when she applied for the job?
What problems do you think she may have faced?

Gondoliers sink hopes of first woman driver

From Martin Penner in Rome

A 35-YEAR-OLD German woman has given up her eight-year battle to enter one of the most exclusive all-male cliques in the world and become Venice's first female gondolier.

Alexandra Hai, from Hamburg, did not pass the basic gondoliering exam for the third time at the weekend, failing to impress a six-person panel. "I gave it my best shot but it's no good. Venice's first female gondolier isn't going to be me," she said disconsolately, abandoning a dream that she had nurtured since moving to the city a decade ago.

Frau Hai works on Venice's water buses and has spent years practising gondoliering.

Gondoliers must steer and row with a single oar from the stern. This requires strength, agility and years of training.

For her exam, Frau Hai was asked to steer a gondola about 800 metres up and down the narrow Rio del Vin. She bumped into another gondola during a previous attempt to pass the 20-minute test, and admitted her performance this time was not faultless.

"There was a bit, under the Ponte dei Greci bridge, when we met a police launch coming the other way and there I didn't manage to hold the boat quite right," she said.

Nevertheless, she believed that she had performed well enough to pass and suggested that she may have been the victim of a desire to keep a foreign woman out of a close-knit masculine world.

She noted that she had to take the test in an area that she did not know very well. "It was always clear that to pass the test I was going to need an absolutely perfect performance, but they always manage to make things difficult for me," she said.

In 1996, after her first attempt, Frau Hai won an appeal on the grounds that there were no women in the examining commission. For both subsequent attempts there have been two.

Franco Vianello Moro, head of Venice's gondola authority, dismissed the suggestion that Frau Hai had been treated with excessive rigour. "Sexism had nothing to do with it," Signor Moro said. "The two women on the commission, both rowing experts, agreed with the judgement that the candidate lacked the necessary ability in a gondola." He said that the strict tests and the limit of 425 on the number of gondoliers were needed to safeguard a unique tradition.

© The Times

Glossary

1 gondolier: the driver of a gondola, a typical boat from Venice
2 the stern: the back of a boat (the bow is the front)
3 a launch: a motor boat
4 sexism: discrimination based on gender

2 As you read, answer the questions to find the meaning of these words.

a If you *give up* your dream, do you abandon it or achieve it?
b Does a *clique* welcome outsiders, or reject them?
c If you *give something your best shot*, do you give up easily or try your hardest?
d Is a *decade* ten years or a hundred years?
e Would you *steer* a boat with an *oar* or a *straw*?
f If you *bump* into something, do you hit it or manage to avoid it?
g If a family or community is *close-knit*, do they get on well or badly?
h If you *dismiss* a suggestion, do you reject or accept it?
i Is a *strict* test easy or difficult?
j Does *safeguard* mean to protect or to threaten?

3 Now circle T (True) or F (False).

a There are now several female gondoliers in Venice. T / F
b Alexandra will keep on taking the test until she passes it. T / F
c For her third test, the panel was made up of three men and two women. T / F
d She has now taken the test four times in all. T / F
e Alexandra has lived in Venice for the past ten years. T / F
f Gondoliers stand on the bow of the boat. T / F
g In one of her previous tests, she hit another gondola. T / F
h The driving test lasts about an hour. T / F
i Alexandra took her third test in an area she was very familiar with. T / F
j The gondola authority admit they are being sexist. T / F
k It is not easy for anybody to be a gondolier. T / F

4 Read and discuss the following.

Use this useful language.
- *It's a fact of life that ...*
- *It's ridiculous that women should be ...*
- *How can you justify* (+ noun or verb + *-ing*)
- *to be biased against/to discriminate against* (=to be prejudiced or unfair)
- *a closed shop* (=a clique that restricts entry to a profession or union)
- *to hit the glass ceiling* (=the idea that women are prevented from getting to the very top of an organisation by an invisible 'ceiling')

a Are there some jobs that women should never do?
b Are there some jobs that men should never do?
c Some people say that 'A woman's place is in the home'. Do you agree or disagree?
d Is there a 'glass ceiling' that makes life difficult for women?
e Should we all just accept that men and women are different and should lead different kinds of lives?

5 Your group have been asked to take part in a radio debate on the topic *It's easier to be a man than a woman*.

a Think of five reasons in favour of this suggestion and five reasons against. Then share your ideas with the rest of the class.

Life is easier for men because ...

-
-
-
-
-

Life is easier for women because ...

-
-
-
-
-

b Now take a class vote to decide if the statement is 'true' or 'false'.

22 The school day

In South Korea, some children study for ten hours a day, six days a week. They have their regular lessons during the day and then, after a short break, they go to special evening schools called *hagwons* for another three or fours hours of classes.

1) Before you read, discuss the following.
How would you feel if you had to go to two different schools every day?
Would you like to study this hard?

Glossary

1 spawned: produced, created
2 cult-like: like a small religious group
3 Organisation of Economic Co-operation and Development (OECD): an international organisation set up to promote trade
4 rounded individuals: well educated people with a wide range of interests

2) As you read, answer the questions to find the meaning of these words.

a Does *drifts* mean moves slowly or moves quickly?
b Does *drooping* mean falling slowly or falling quickly?
c Does *scribbles* mean writes slowly and clearly or writes quickly and not very neatly?
d Does *outlaw* mean forbid or encourage?
e Does *catch up with* mean be jealous of or reach the same standard as?
f Does *go without* mean sacrifice or insist on?
g Does *entrenched* mean unimportant or deep-rooted?
h Does *skip* mean concentrate on or forget about?
i Does *fanatical* mean too casual or too serious?
j Does *prosperity* mean poverty or wealth?

3) Now complete these sentences with words or information from the article.

a About _____ % of Korean students go to *hagwons*.
b Yang Dong-myung studies _____ hours a night, _____ nights a week.
c A new law will force *hagwons* to finish teaching by _____ pm.
d South Korea has the _____ largest economy in Asia.
e The country has few _____ resources such as minerals, oil and gas.
f International studies place 15-year-old Koreans first in science and _____ in mathematics.
g It costs about $_____ a week to send your child to night school.
h Lee Sook is willing to go without _____ if it means her children can go to a *hagwon*.
i On the day of the annual university entrance exam, offices start work an _____ late and airports restrict _____ and _____ to help students concentrate.
j Lee Nan-young wants her children to do more _____ and have more _____ .

4) Now discuss the following.

a Are there similar schools to *hagwons* in your country? Would you like to go to one? Why/Why not?
b Why do we go to school? What is education for?
c Are there things you should not learn at school, but should learn from your family and friends? For example, who should teach you about politics/sex education/how to deal with money/religion/the risks from smoking or taking drugs?
d What makes a good school?

5) Your group have been asked to plan a new school for 200 children aged seven to 11. Give your new school a name and then decide the following.

- class size?
- mixed or single-sex?
- school uniform?
- what subjects will be taught?
- balance of fun and study?
- how long will the lessons be?
- starting and finishing time of school?
- how many breaks?
- school rules?

Now present your new school to the rest of the class.

Lessons leave no time for play in Seoul

Andrew Ward on the South Korean education system where fierce competition has spawned an $11bn-a-year private evening school industry.

A 17-year-old boy drifts into sleep, his head drooping into the textbook open in front of him. It is 9pm and Yang Dong-myung has two more hours of study to complete before going home. Around him sit other teenage South Koreans struggling to stay awake as a tutor scribbles English vocabulary on a blackboard.

Mr Yang and his classmates are among the roughly 80 per cent of South Koreans who attend private evening schools, known as *hagwon*, to improve their chances of reaching university.

An almost cult-like devotion to learning has been among the driving forces behind South Korea's rapid economic development over the past half century, creating one of the world's most highly educated workforces.

But concern is growing that the obsession with education has spun out of control, putting children under too much stress and families under pressure to pay expensive tuition fees.

The government signalled its alarm last month by announcing plans to outlaw evening classes after 10pm as part of tougher regulation of the $11bn (€8.6bn, £5.8bn) *hagwon* industry.

Mr Yang attends his *hagwon* in Seoul four evenings a week from 6pm to 11pm after a full day at school. "I get tired and fall asleep in class," he says. "But in Korea education is important so my parents force me to study."

South Korea spends 6.8 per cent of gross domestic product on education, more that any other member of the Organisation for Economic Co-operation and Development. However, the country's public spending on education is below the OECD average at 4.1 per cent, highlighting the role played by private tuition in Asia's fourth-largest economy.

The teachings of Confucius, the ancient Chinese philosopher who stressed the importance of scholarship, influence many east Asian societies.

In South Korea, the zeal for learning is reinforced by a belief that knowledge is crucial to the bid to catch up with richer nations such as Japan and stay ahead of China.

"Korea is a country with few natural resources so to better ourselves individually and as a nation we have to use our brains," say Lee Nan-young, mother of two teenage students.

Commitment to education is reflected by research showing South Korea's 15-year-olds have the highest scientific literacy and second-highest mathematics standards among OECD members.

A slogan on the classroom wall in Mr Yang's English lesson reads: "Accomplish your dreams". But dreams come at a price: in his *hagwon*, fees of $280 a week.

"Half of our family's income is spent on education," says Lee Sook, mother of two *hagwon* students. "We go without holidays to afford it. In every area of life we make sacrifices for our children's education."

Lee Hang-soo, vice-president of Mr Yang's *hagwon*, says the school grants bursaries to children from poor families. But he admits South Korea's education system is divisive: "The 20 per cent of children that don't attend *hagwon* are split between those that can't afford it and those clever enough not to need it."

Private tuition has become so entrenched that public schools skip parts of the curriculum on the assumption it will be taught in evening classes.

"Public education teaches students to be rounded individuals; *hagwon* exist to get them through the university entrance exam," says Mr Lee.

Getting into a good university is considered a ticket to success in status conscious South Korea, where people are judged according to educational background.

The annual entrance exam is so important that people start work an hour late on test day to keep roads clear for candidates, while airports restrict take-offs and landings during the exam to avoid disturbing students.

However, there is growing awareness of the negative consequence of such a fanatical approach to education.

"I worry about my children having no time to exercise and have fun," says Lee Nan-young. "Children are getting fat because they are always studying."

Jung Bong-sup, head of school policy at the ministry of education, says the *hagwon* style of teaching fails to provide the skills needed in the modern global economy.

"Students memorise facts but they don't learn the ideas behind them," he says. "In the 21st century people need to think creatively and that requires more interactive education."

However as long as university remains the path to prosperity in South Korea, parents will send their children to *hagwon*. "If other kids go then so must yours," says Mrs Lee.

© Financial Times

23 Bullies at school

Bullying has always been a problem in British schools. This article describes a campaign by The Daily Mirror newspaper and a charity called Kidscape to try and encourage children to talk openly about how bullies and bullying can change the atmosphere of a school.

1 Before you read, discuss the following.
What sort of things do bullies do? Give some examples. Can you think of ways that bullies can be stopped?

Glossary

1 Childline: a charity that operates a special phone line that children can call for help and advice 24 hours a day
2 pick on: bully, attack, treat unfairly
3 not getting anywhere: failing, not achieving anything
4 put off: discourage; stop

2 As you read, match the words from the article 1–10 with their meanings a–j.

1 at some point	a)	increase, strengthen, make better
2 dreadful	b)	strong
3 deter	c)	suggestions, ideas, advice
4 tips	d)	will probably be
5 boost	e)	really bad, horrible, disgusting
6 become resigned to	f)	at some time, eventually
7 hunched	g)	discourage, put off
8 firm	h)	bent; not standing up straight
9 is likely to	i)	stay with
10 stick with	j)	start accepting

3 Choose the best answer.

a According to the article ...
(1) about a million children are bullied at UK schools.
(2) bullying can cause long-term damage.
(3) 20,000 parents call Kidscape every year.
b Kidscape ...
(1) runs special courses for children who have been bullied.
(2) is an an international charity.
(3) gets 16,000 calls a year from children.
c The charity suggests that ...
(1) you should not tell anyone if you are being bullied.
(2) you must never walk away from a bully.
(3) you should stand up straight and look the bully in the eye.
d Bullies ...
(1) pick on strong, self confident people.
(2) get really angry if you repeat a statement.
(3) love to get a reaction from you.

4 Now discuss the following.

a Have you ever been bullied? If so, what happened? How did you feel?
b Have you ever been a bully yourself? If so, what happened? How did you feel?
c Have you ever seen bullying? Did you interfere or walk away?
d Why do people bully others? What do they gain from it?
e What effect does bullying have? Does it make bullied people stronger and ready for the real world?
f Would a bully be good at any particular job?
g What can we do to stop bullying?

5 Your group have been asked to design an anti-bullying poster that will appear on school noticeboards around the country.

a Make some rough sketches of what the poster might look like. As you develop your ideas, think about these things.
- What is your message? What do you want to say?
- Are you talking to the bullies, the victims or both?
- What is the best way to get your message across? A slogan? A few simple words? Or a headline followed by lots of information?
- There will be other posters on the noticeboards. So how can you make your poster stand out and get noticed?

b Now make a final copy of the poster to show the rest of the class.
c Present your poster to the rest of the class. Explain your ideas and get some feedback. How would the class react to a poster like this?

To find out more about The Daily Mirror campaign, go to www.kidscape.org.uk and www.childline.org.uk

YOU DON'T HAVE TO BE A PLAYGROUND VICTIM

12 WAYS TO BEAT BULLIES

It's an ugly, cruel and unnecessary part of school life and is a source of misery for millions of children.

More than two million youngsters in the UK are bullied at some point in their school years. Of these, 40 per cent suffer bullying twice a week or more.

Childline receives about 20,000 calls a year from bullied youngsters while the charity Kidscape gets about 16,000 phone calls from the worried parents of bullied children.

One in 12 youngsters are bullied so badly it affects their education, relationships and even their job prospects in later life.

And in 10 to 15 cases every year the bullying reaches such a dreadful level that it drives the young victims to suicide.

This week the Daily Mirror's Beat the Bullies campaign has been looking at ways to eradicate the problem.

Today we offer 12 practical ideas for youngsters to deter bullies, plus five tips from children who have experienced bullying, to help children keep themselves safe and boost their confidence.

These clever methods are taught on special courses for bullied children run by Kidscape, the only national charity dedicated to beating bullying.

1. BY law, schools must have a way of dealing with bullying. Use your school's anti-bullying policy to get help and if you're not sure how it works, talk to your teacher or headteacher.
   Don't become resigned to being a victim. You CAN help yourself and get others to help you.

2. TELL a friend what is happening. It will be harder for the bully to pick on you if you have a pal with you for support.

3. TRY to ignore the bully or say "No!" really firmly, then walk away. Don't worry if people think you are running away – it is very hard for the bully to go on picking on someone who won't stand still to listen to their threats.

4. MOST bullied children have negative body language – hunched up and looking at the floor. Try to stand straight and make eye contact with people.

5. IF you don't want to do something, don't give in to pressure. Be firm. Remember, everyone has the right to say no.

6. SIMPLY repeat a statement again and again: "No, you can't have my lunch money, no, you can't have my lunch money!" The bully will get bored because they are not getting anywhere and give up.

7. MAKE your phrase short and precise: Say "It's my pencil." or "Go away" firmly.

8. DON'T show that you are upset or angry. Bullies love to get a reaction – it's "fun". Keep calm and hide your emotions – the bully might get bored and leave you alone.

9. MAKE up funny or clever replies in advance. They don't have to be brilliant, but it helps to have an answer ready. Practise saying them at home. If the bully says: "Give me your sweets," you could say: "OK, but my dog licked them so they don't taste very nice."

10. AVOID being alone in places where you know the bully is likely to be. This might mean changing your route to school, or avoiding certain parts of the playground, or only using toilets when other people are there. It's not fair, but it might put the bully off. Remember, your safety is the most important thing to consider.

11. STOP thinking like a victim. If you have been bullied for a long time, you might start to believe what the bully says – that you're ugly, awful and no one will ever like you. This is "victim-think".

12. MAKE a list of all the good things you can think of about yourself. Talk to yourself in a positive way. Say: "I may not look like a film star, but I'm good at maths and have a brilliant sense of humour."

KIDS' CODE   KIDS' CODE   KIDS' CODE

PRACTISE walking tall. Bullies pick on people they think are weak. If you look confident, the bully is less likely to pick on you.

STICK with a group – even if they are not really your friends. Bullies tend to pick on people when they are on their own.

KEEP a diary about what is happening. A written record of the bullying makes it much easier to prove what has been going on.

DON'T fight back if you can help it. You could make the situation worse, get hurt or even be blamed for starting the trouble.

IT'S not worth getting hurt over a possession. You may have to give bullies what they want. Property can be replaced – you can't.

© Daily Mirror

24 New foods

Sweet strawmato is pick of the crop

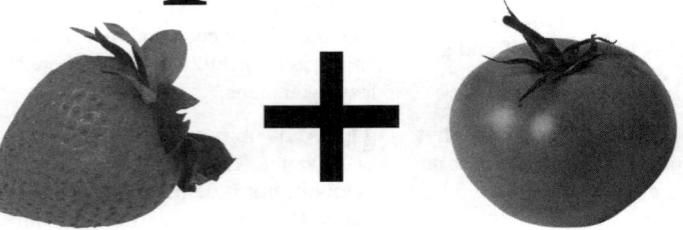

M&S says its new fruit hybrid is perfect for dipping in chocolate

BY JONATHAN PRYNN
Consumer Affairs Editor

THEY may not be serving it with cream at Wimbledon just yet, but a new variety of tomato is bidding to rival soft fruit in the nation's summer affections.

The so-called strawmato is one of the sweetest tomatoes ever developed. It has been designed to be perfect for dipping, just like a strawberry.

Growers in Lancashire have crossed tomato varieties to give the strawmato a distinctive pointed end – making it look uncannily like England's favourite summer treat.

It has been designed in response to growing demand for ever sweeter and more varied types of tomato from British consumers. The strawmato is judged by growers to be twice as sweet as standard tomatoes.

Marks & Spencer, which has an exclusive deal to stock the strawmato, hopes that consumers will follow America, where it is now fashionable to dip sweet tomatoes in chocolate. The store also hope they will be eaten as a healthy alternative to sweet snacks.

It is also stocking an even sweeter tomato – dubbed the "ugly tomato" because of its extraordinary dark green skin and wrinkled appearance.

The strawmato is still officially "under wraps" and is not expected to go on sale until next summer after a final round of tweaks to its taste "profile".

Bernard Sparkes, development executive at Geest, the food company developing the strawmato, said: "We want sweetness but with a balance. If it is too sweet it can be sickly."

Marks & Spencer fruit buyer Peter Ireland said: "People are getting more adventurous and want to try different varieties of tomato. They want tomatoes that look unusual and exciting to put in the salad bowl. The strawberry tomato looks fantastic and it has a great taste – it can be eaten on its own or in salad."

M&S claims to be one of the pioneers of unusual tomatoes in Britain, first selling cherry tomatoes in the Seventies. The company's food stores stock 20 varieties of tomato, although it has slimmed down the range since its chief executive said that customers were getting too confused by too much choice. The traditional tomato now accounts for less than half the 75,000 tonnes of tomatoes grown in Britain each year.

Meanwhile, importers warn that tomatoes could be in short supply this summer because snow storms in southern Spain wreaked havoc with the country's crop. Spain and the Canary Islands supply almost half of Britain's total consumption of 420,000 tonnes a year.

FEAST OF FRUITY NEW VARIETIES

- "Purple Haze" carrot. A purple variety available in Sainsbury's
- Purple peppers. A sweet variety of pepper on sale at some Sainsbury's outlets
- "Kutamo". A black variety of tomato from the Galapagos Islands, on sale at some Sainsbury's outlets
- Golden beetroot, sold by Waitrose
- Round courgette. A cricket-ball sized courgette sold in Sainsbury's
- Round carrot, developed to appeal to children, sold in Waitrose
- White cucumber: firm and juicy cucumber with a non-bitter skin, sold in Sainsbury's

© Evening Standard

NEWSPAPER ARTICLES TO GET TEENAGERS TALKING — Food and health

If you go into a British supermarket, you may be surprised by some of the foods on display. Some of them sell black tomatoes, white cucumbers and carrots that are purple or round. This article looks at another new product called the strawmato, a tomato that looks and tastes like a strawberry.

1 Before you read, discuss the following.

Would you like to try a strawmato, a black tomato or a purple carrot?

Do you think these new foods are just harmless and fun, or are they unnatural and perhaps even dangerous?

Glossary

1 the pick of: the best of
2 a hybrid: a combination of two things
3 Wimbledon: strawberries and cream is the traditional dessert eaten at the Wimbledon tennis championships
4 Marks & Spencer (M&S), Sainsbury's, Waitrose: major supermarkets
5 under wraps: top secret
6 tweaks: very small adjustments
7 wreaked havoc: caused chaos

2 As you read, match the words from the article 1–10 with their meanings a–j.

1 bidding		a)	much too sweet
2 dipping		b)	top secret
3 uncannily		c)	not enough, a shortage
4 standard		d)	called, named, nicknamed
5 dubbed		e)	attempting, trying
6 wrinkled		f)	not smooth
7 under wraps		g)	putting in
8 sickly		h)	typical, normal, traditional
9 accounts for		i)	unbelievably, amazingly
10 in short supply		j)	makes up, is

3 Choose the best answer.

a The Strawmato ...
 (1) is a cross between a strawberry and a potato.
 (2) is half as sweet as a standard tomato.
 (3) looks like a strawberry.
b The so-called 'ugly tomato' ...
 (1) is light green.
 (2) is sweeter than a strawmato.
 (3) has a smooth skin.
c Marks & Spencer ...
 (1) began selling cherry tomatoes in the 1980s.
 (2) now stocks 30 varieties of tomatoes.
 (3) says customers like exciting foods.
d Spain ...
 (1) was hit by a series of floods.
 (2) provides 90% of Britain's tomatoes.
 (3) produced fewer tomatoes this year.
e Sainsbury's sells ...
 (1) a purple carrot.
 (2) a blue tomato.
 (3) an orange cucumber.
f Waitrose is now selling ...
 (1) a brown beetroot.
 (2) a square banana.
 (3) a round carrot.

4 Now discuss the following.

a Is it safe to create new foods like the strawmato in a laboratory?
b Environmental campaigners claim that we are creating 'Frankenstein food' with dangerous long-term implications. Do you agree?
c GM (genetically modified) crops produce more food from a smaller area of land. Is it good to do this to feed more people? Or should we ban all GM food?
d Do you ever read the labels on packets of food? Do you understand the information given? Do you care what is in your food?
e Is it right to put pesticides or sprays on crops, or should all food be organic?
f Do you ever buy organic food? Why is it more expensive than non-organic food? Would you buy it if it were cheaper?
g Should we trust scientists who say that these new foods are safe?

5 In groups, come up with a new kind of food. Describe its taste and appearance and explain why it would be popular.

a Present your new product to the rest of the class using the language below.

We've created a new kind of food called a _____ .

What is different about it is that it is _____ .

It has an unusual appearance. It is _____ with _____ .

It tastes (more/less) _____ .

This product will appeal to _____ and people will buy it because _____ .

Well, that's our product. What do you think of it?

b The other groups now vote on whether this product should be made or not. They should say why/why not.

NEWSPAPER ARTICLES TO GET TEENAGERS TALKING — Food and health

25 Too old to have children?

With new medical techniques, it is now possible for a woman to get pregnant in her 60s. In 2005, a lady in Romania gave birth at the age of 67. This article appeared in an American newspaper after a 59-year old businesswoman had twins at a private clinic in London. The British Health Minister, Virginia Bottomley, said that 59 was too old to have a child, but others disagreed.

1 Before you read, discuss the following.
Is it right for women to have children in their 50s and 60s? What problems may they face?

Glossary

1 Health Secretary: the Health Minister
2 barb: criticism
3 a fertility clinic: a special hospital to help women get pregnant
4 a Caesarian section: delivering the baby after cutting the mother's stomach
5 crack: a type of cocaine
6 fetal alcohol syndrome: problems babies get if their mothers drink alocohol when pregnant
7 a test tube baby: a baby conceived by in-vitro fertilisation (IVF)
8 charge up: inspire

Note: The article uses American English spellings fetal, program and fertilization. In UK English these are spelled foetal, programme and fertilisation.

2 As you read, answer the questions to find the meaning of these words.

a Does *endure* mean enjoy or suffer?
b Does *stirring up* mean creating or rejecting?
c Are *physicians* doctors or people who study physics?
d Is a *dropout* someone who stays in school or someone who leaves school?
e Does *skipping* mean doing or not doing?
f Does *costly* mean cheap or expensive?
g Does *the odds are* mean probably or probably not?
h Does *tightfisted* mean generous or mean?
i Does *impaired* mean damaged or healthy?
j Does *cut short* mean stopped early or extended?

3 Now circle T (True) or F (False).

a The businesswoman gave birth to twins in a hospital in Rome. T / F
b British doctors refused to treat her because she was poor. T / F
c Her family have helped her. T / F
d The British Health Minister wants to ban such treatment. T / F
e Drinking alcohol while pregnant can put your child at risk. T / F
f A pregnant woman can pass AIDS on to her unborn child. T / F
g IVF treatment is very expensive and often unsuccessful. T / F
h An Italian senator wants to ban IVF treatment for teenage girls. T / F
i Dr Antinori's 63-year-old patient is having her first child. T / F
j The writer thinks more should be done to stop some younger mothers from having babies. T / F

4 Now discuss the following.

a Now that you have read the article, have you changed your mind about women having babies in their 50s and 60s?
b Is it OK for men to become fathers in their 50s and 60s? Why/Why not?
c The writer says that some young mothers are 'unsuitable'. Do you agree?
d What problems do some girls have if they get pregnant at a very young age?
e What will happen if parents can choose the sex of their baby? Is this a good thing?
f Should we stop scientific research into controversial areas like cloning and genetic engineering? Can science go too far, or is it always a good thing?

5 You have been asked to take part in a radio programme called *How science has changed the world*. Divide into two groups, one for science and one against science.

- One group should think of five examples of how science has made the world a better place.
- One group should think of five examples of how science has made it worse.

Present your arguments. Take a class vote. Is science good or bad?

Older Mom Not So Bad

By Joan Beck

"Women do not have the right to have a child. The child has a right to a suitable home." British Health Secretary Virginia Bottomley may have a point. But she aimed her barb at the wrong target – the 59-year old woman who gave birth to twins in a London hospital on Christmas Day. The oldest new mother on record, she had donor eggs, implanted in a fertility clinic in Rome, after British doctors refused to treat her because of her age.

Identified only as a wealthy businesswoman married to a 45-year-old economist, the mother is described as healthy and financially secure, with a supportive family. Why shouldn't she have a baby if she wants one enough to endure the infertility treatments, the pregnancy and a Caesarean section?

But Bottomley and others have wasted no time stirring up criticism and controversy about the babies. The health secretary is talking about conferring with other countries about "ethical controls" that would prevent the use of such infertility treatments for older women, even if they pay the costs themselves and do not involve government health programs.

Other British physicians and politicians are publicly calling for new laws throughout Europe to ban pregnancies among older women.

What has the woman done that merits such ethical concern and public criticism? She isn't an unmarried, 15-year-old high school dropout whose unplanned baby will put her on welfare, perhaps for decades. She isn't 21 and having her fourth baby by four men, none of whom will actively father their children.

She hasn't been using crack or other illegal drugs during pregnancy, condemning her unborn infant to neurological problems of unpredictable severity. She's not passing along the AIDS virus or forcing fetal alcohol syndrome on her child by her drinking. She's not risking her baby's health by skipping prenatal care.

Her twins aren't the unintended and unwanted consequence of careless sex. They are the result of a long, costly, difficult effort to have children long after childbearing seemed biologically impossible. She may not have as much energy as a younger mother. She may not live long enough to see her children's children. (Surely it is evidence of sexual bias that these arguments are made only about woman, not about men who become fathers in their 50s or 60s.)

But the odds are her twins will be more likely to have a "suitable home" than tens of thousands of babies born this year in the United States and Britain.

Bottomley and other critics may have an argument about limiting the use of expensive and often unsuccessful test-tube baby services provided by Britain's tightfisted national health plan to younger women where chances of failure may be less. (Britain rations some other kinds of costly health care by age.)

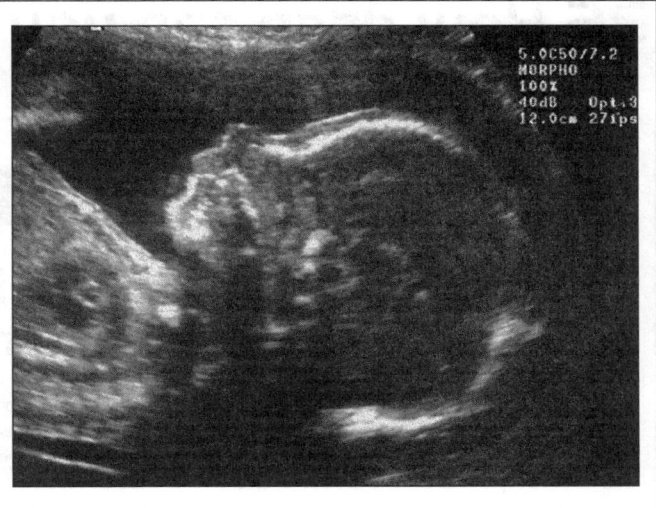

But zeal for saving the British money shouldn't lead these opponents to try to influence treatment available in other nations or to stop women from using their own money for the fertility treatment they want.

The fuss has already spread to Italy where a senator, who is also a gynaecologist, has introduced legislation that would forbid the use of such in-vitro fertilizations for older women. The most visible target for this outburst of self-righteous ethical concern is the Italian fertility doctor Severino Antinori, who helped the British mother become pregnant. One of his current patients, who is now three months pregnant, will be 63 when she gives birth. She and her husband, who is a year older, decided to try to have another child after their teenage son was killed in a traffic accident.

Of course a baby should be entitled to a "suitable home," to a mother and a father who are actively involved in his care and have the maturity and resources to provide for his needs and to give him the best possible start in life. Most of all, he should be entitled to be wanted and loved.

But there is no reason to assume that the British mother and her husband or the Italian couple or any of the other postmenopausal women who have given birth or are now pregnant will not provide a suitable home.

There is great reason, however, for Bottomley and her colleagues to be concerned about the babies being born all over the world without suitable homes or caring, able, energetic parents.

What can be done about women who won't – or can't – stop using crack or other illegal drugs or alcohol during pregnancy and imposing known risk on their unborn offspring? What kind of suitable home will such women provide for a baby, who may be born already impaired?

Why not devote more ethical concern to mothers who are too young instead of too old, to young teenagers who are too immature even to care for themselves well, who have cut short their education and cut off their job prospects, who do not or cannot provide their offspring with an active and involved father? Many of these babies, by default, will essentially be raised by their grandmothers, who may not only be short of energy but of basic resources.

If Bottomley wants to charge up her counterparts in other nations to take on these ethical concerns, she may be able to accomplish far more than she can by trying to prevent a few pregnancies in older women.

© International Herald Tribune

26 How deep can you go?

The human submarine

400ft below the Atlantic, British diver achieves a breathtaking world record

By Jacqui Goddard on Providenciales Islands

TANYA STREETER took one almighty breath and went under the water.

Down into the Atlantic Ocean she went, going even deeper than submarines could once reach.

At 400ft – unaided by any breathing apparatus – she had reached her target.

By any standards, her achievement had been breathtaking.

By the time she resurfaced, the British diver had been holding her breath for three minutes and 38 seconds.

But, more significantly, the 30-year-old had set a new world freediving record, going deeper than anyone in the history of the sport.

She had smashed the previous best by a woman by a staggering 88.3ft. She had also beaten the men's best by 6.3ft, making her the only woman in any sport to have beaten a male world record.

"It won't sink in until I've read about it, but for now I think we can say it feels good," she said.

The former pupil at Roedean College in Sussex celebrated with champagne on Monday after her feat off the Turks and Caicos Islands.

Miss Streeter, named 'the world's most perfect athlete' by America's Sports Illustrated magazine, was lowered to 400ft on a metal sled attached to a cable.

Safety divers, at 60ft intervals down, tapped signals to her to let her know her depth, and after reaching the target she swam away and kicked to the surface under her own power. "I heard the divers say 'It's a new world record', but they were on helium, so they had high-pitched voices."

As she came up, she winked at her husband Paul who had dived down to accompany her the last 70ft.

Miss Streeter is able to go six minutes without breathing. By developing unique exercises to expand the rib cage – displacing her heart by several inches – she can fill her lungs with about 50 per cent more air than the average person.

"As a freediver I am using about 80 to 100 percent of my lung capacity. When you breathe normally it's only about 30," she said.

When freediving, the heartbeat slows to a quarter of its usual rate. The water pressure squashes the lungs to the size of an orange and the circulatory system goes into partial shutdown. The greatest risk is that the diver may pass out at depth.

The inability to exhale also causes carbon dioxide to build up in the body, meaning thoughts become incoherent. But Miss Streeter said: "Touch wood, I have never had evidence of any damage to my lungs. Whenever I am looked at by doctors, I am told I have the lungs of a 15-year old."

She added: "There was a time when even submarines couldn't go as deep as I went. But I have never seen it as a case of conquering the depths or beating the sea. I look at it as a privilege to be accepted in such a way by nature's most powerful force."

Miss Streeter, who was born in the Cayman Islands to a British mother and American father, graduated from Brighton University with a degree in public administration and French.

She married Paul, from Brighton, in 1995 and now lives in Austin, Texas.

Her achievements have brought attention from medical researchers. But she said yesterday: "Actually, I consider myself quite a coward. I'd be scared witless to go halfway up Everest."

Factfile
Equipment: Weighted sled attached to winch
Descent: More than 6ft a second
Duration: Descent lasts one minute Whole record took 3 mins 38secs

Below 200ft: Pressure on eardrums needs equalising. Heart rate 60 bpm

Past 300ft: In constant pain. Chest so compressed her wetsuit feels two sizes too big. Heart rate 20bpm

400ft: NEW WORLD RECORD for diver returning to surface under own power

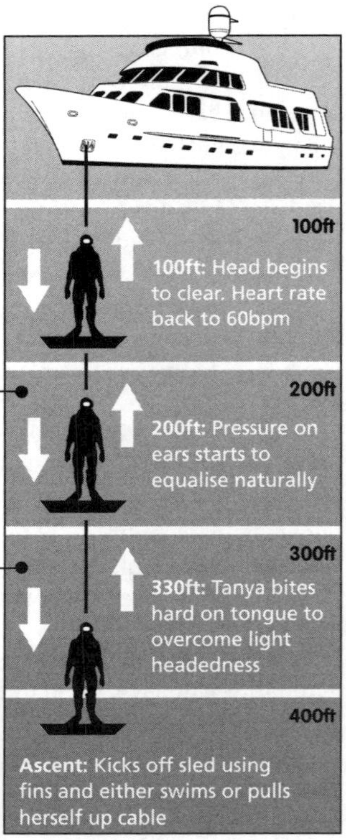

100ft: Head begins to clear. Heart rate back to 60bpm

200ft: Pressure on ears starts to equalise naturally

330ft: Tanya bites hard on tongue to overcome light headedness

Ascent: Kicks off sled using fins and either swims or pulls herself up cable

Tanya with husband Paul.

© The Daily Mail

NEWSPAPER ARTICLES TO GET TEENAGERS TALKING — Food and health

This article is about an extraordinary diver called Tanya Streeter. In July 2003, she stood on a small platform tied to a rope, and was pulled down towards the bottom of the ocean. At 120 metres down, the platform stopped and she swam back to the surface. The whole dive took a total of 218 seconds. Incredibly, she did this without an oxygen mask, just using the air from a single breath.

1) Before you read, discuss the following.

What would it be like to try a dive like this, 120 metres down on a single breath of air? What would happen to your body? How would you feel?

Glossary

1. 400 ft (feet): just under 122 metres
2. Roedean College: a famous private school
3. a sled: the platform she stands on at the beginning of the dive
4. to be scared witless: to be really frightened
5. mins: minutes
6. secs: seconds
7. bpm: beats per minutes

2) As you read, complete the puzzle using words from the article.

1. equipment
2. broke (a record) by a big margin
3. a person who swims under water
4. at 120 metres down, Tanya's heart beat slows to a quarter of its usual _____
5. breathe out
6. make bigger
7. Tanya can dive to a _____ of 120 metres.
8. The other divers breathe _____ which makes their voices high.
9. *Sports Illustrated* is one of many _____ that has written about her.
10. Water pressure _____ the lungs to the size of an orange.
11. underwater 'ships'
12. a platform that carries Tanya down into the water
13. When you don't exhale, carbon _____ builds up in the body.

Crossword down clues: 1 A, 2 S, 3 D, 4 R, 5 E, 6 E, 7 D
Crossword across starting letters: 8 H, 9 M, 10 S, 11 S, 12 S, 13 D

3) Now circle T (True) or F (False).

a. Tanya can dive deeper than any man. T / F
b. The sled is made of soft wood. T / F
c. Safety divers give her information using special radios. T / F
d. Helium makes your voice sound deeper. T / F
e. Tanya does special exercises to make her rib cage bigger. T / F
f. As you dive down, your heart rate increases. T / F
g. As you dive down, your lungs get smaller. T / F
h. Some divers faint when they are deep under water. T / F
i. A build-up of carbon dioxide helps you to think clearly. T / F
j. Tanya now wants to go up Everest. T / F

4) Now discuss the following.

a. Is Tanya Streeter brave or crazy?
b. Why do people take risks like this? What do they get out of it?
c. What do you feel about other 'extreme' sports such as hang gliding, white water rafting, bunjee jumping, parachuting and rock climbing?
d. Should any of these sports be banned? Why/Why not?

5) A radio programme has asked you to describe the most dangerous or scariest thing you have ever done. Write your answer with the other members of your group using the phrases below.

The most dangerous/scariest thing I've ever done was ...
What happened was ...
I felt ... because ...
I would/wouldn't do it again because ...

Now present your stories to the rest of the class. Have a vote to decide which thing was the most dangerous or most scary.

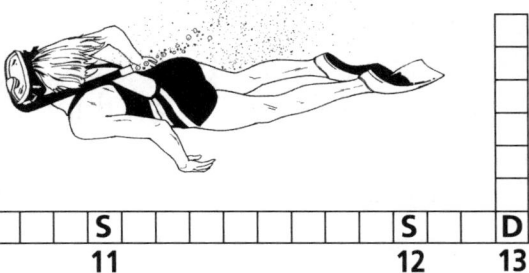

27 Better school meals

iPod lure to cut down junk food

Healthy eating school pupils in Glasgow are to be rewarded with iPods and Xbox consoles for ditching junk food.

Glasgow City Council is offering the electronic incentives to about 30,000 children in 29 secondary schools.

The pupils are given swipecards and can claim various prizes depending on the number of points they gain for eating "sensibly" on school premises.

A council spokeswoman said youngsters "wouldn't turn up their noses at winning an iPod for eating nice food".

They can redeem their points for a selection of goods – from cinema tickets and book tokens to top-of-the-range iPods and Xbox games consoles – at the end of the term.

The council spokeswoman said the scheme, which involves pupils signing up on a voluntary basis, encouraged them to stay within school boundaries at breaks and lunchtimes.

"It means there will be less temptation to go to the chip shop or McDonald's," she said.

"There are a variety of healthy choices on the menu and most pupils wouldn't turn up their noses at winning an iPod for eating nice food."

It would take 100 meals worth 40 points to reach the 4,000 points required for an iPod.

"The most popular thing on the menu is a Vital Mix, which includes soup, a filled pitta, yoghurt and healthy drink like milk, so it's not a case of just lettuce leaves and water," the spokeswoman went on.

"The reward for the Vital Mix, which costs £1.15, is 40 points, so it would take just 100 of these to get an iPod."

"The swipecard has the pupil's photo on it and the dinner ladies who swipe them obviously know who is who."

The scheme was piloted in three schools in Glasgow at the beginning of last year and is now operating in all of the city's secondary schools.

It will cost the council £40,000 a year - but the local authority said it was a small price to pay if it encouraged children to eat better food which would have a lasting effect on their health.

> "We would prefer to incentify the scheme rather than be seen as people who ban things"
> Steven Purcell
> Glasgow City Council

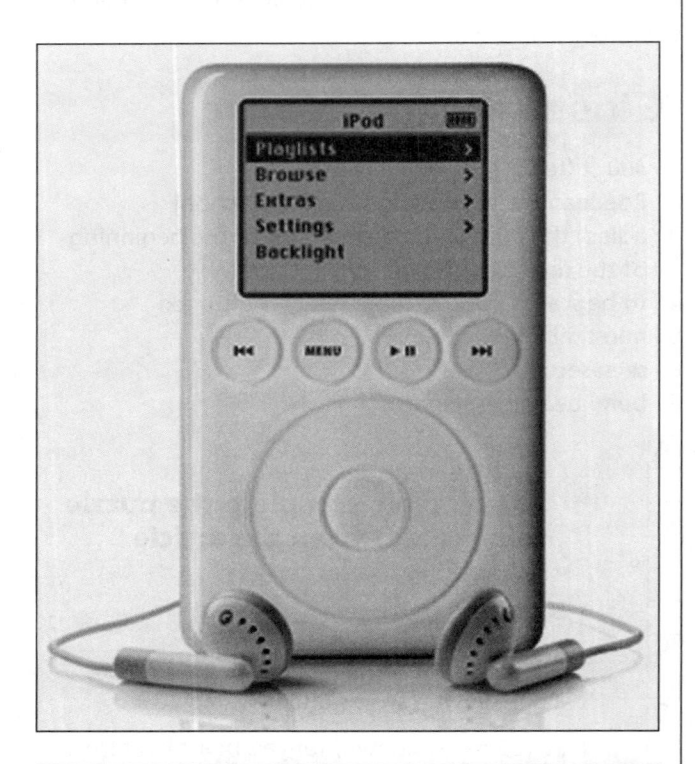

HEALTHY EATING REWARD CARD

iPod - **4,000 points**

Xbox - **3,000 points**

£10 Amazon voucher - **1,500 points**

Pair of cinema tickets - **850 points**

Pasta, salad tub, green salad, breakfast cereal - **15 points**

Steven Purcell, the council's education convener and chairman of the health and diet working group, said he hoped children would be drawn to the scheme.

"We would prefer to incentify the scheme rather than be seen as people who ban things," he said.

"I think we have to recognise that with all the advertising that goes on in schools, the challenge is actually quite hard for us."

And he added: "We have an appalling health record in Glasgow and we need to try anything that will turn that around and make a lasting difference."

© BBC NEWS

NEWSPAPER ARTICLES TO GET TEENAGERS TALKING   Food and health

Most British children have a hot lunch at school and can choose what they eat from a range of dishes in a canteen. As you might expect, when pupils are given a choice between junk food and healthy food, most of them choose chips, burgers and milkshakes. To promote healthier eating, the city council in Glasgow have decided to encourage children to change the way they eat in an unusual way.

1 Before you read, discuss the following.
Do you prefer fast food to healthy food?
What could a council or school do to make children give up junk food and have a healthier diet?

Glossary

1 iPod: a tiny computer storing hundreds of songs or video clips
2 lure: reward, incentive, prize
3 cut down: reduce
4 Xbox: a computer games player
5 swipecard: a plastic card that stores information
6 turn up their noses at: reject, not be interested in
7 Amazon: an internet bookshop
8 dinner ladies: the women working in the school canteen

2 As you read, complete the puzzle using words from the article.

Across
7 terrible, really bad
8 reward, incentive, prize
9 long term, permanent
10 abandoning, getting rid of, giving up

Down
1 a type of healthy, flat bread
2 rubbish, poor quality, not healthy
3 850 points earns you a .... of cinema tickets.
4 The new scheme was .... (=tried out, tested) in three schools.
5 A green .... may include lettuce and cucumber.
6 forbid

3 Now choose the best answer.
a Under the Glasgow scheme ...
  (1) only meals eaten on the school premises earn points.
  (2) every pupil is forced to have a swipecard.
  (3) the iPods and Xboxes available are of poor quality.
b The Vital Mix option ...
  (1) earns you 15 points.
  (2) is the least popular thing on the menu.
  (3) includes soup, bread and yoghurt.
c The healthy eating scheme ...
  (1) was piloted in five schools.
  (2) operates in all Glasgow's primary schools.
  (3) costs the council £40,000 a year.
d Steven Purcell ...
  (1) wants to give children incentives to eat well.
  (2) says it will be easy to change the way children eat.
  (3) thinks Glasgow has a good health record.

4 Now discuss the following.
a What do you think of the Glasgow 'healthy eating' scheme?
b Would you eat 100 healthy school meals to get an iPod or an XBox?
c Is junk food really bad? Or is it a tasty, fun alternative to healthy food? Why is junk food so popular?
d Should junk food companies be allowed to advertise near schools or during television programmes watched by children?
e What is your favourite food? Why do you like it so much?

5 Your local council have decided to introduce a similar 'healthy eating scheme' in schools in your area. They have asked your group to come up with some recommendations.

a Think of a suitable healthy menu.
b Think of a list of rewards to encourage children to eat well.
c Present your suggestions to the rest of the class. Use the following language.

Our healthy eating menu would include ...
We wouldn't allow foods like ...
The rewards would be ...
To earn our top prize of ..., the children would have to eat ...
Our healthy eating scheme would be a good idea because ...

Have a class vote on the best healthy eating scheme.

28 The 12-year-old alcoholic

This is an article about Sherrie Cooke, who became an alcoholic at the age of 12. For the next four years, she spent her nights drinking. She gave up school and her life was in a mess. Then, at 16, Sherrie turned things around and she won a scholarship to study in America. This article appeared in The Sun on the day that a television documentary told her story.

1 Before you read, discuss the following.
Are you surprised that a 12-year-old child could become an alcoholic?
At what age (if any) should you be able to drink:
(a) wine? (b) beer? (c) spirits?

---

11 ALCOPOPS, 4 PINTS OF STELLA, FIVE BUBBLEGUM SHOTS AND A BOTTLE OF VODKA ... ALL IN ONE NIGHT

BINGE DRINKER AGED 12

by Jacqui Thornton

BINGE-DRINKING girl Sherrie Cooke has revealed the shocking rate of booze she used to sink in ONE NIGHT after getting hooked on alcohol aged just 12.

She began boozing with pals and got steadily worse over four years – regularly ending up in a helpless drunken stupor.

A typical night's intake included 11 alcopops, 4½ pints of Stella Artois lager, five bubblegum-flavoured vodka shots and a quarter bottle of vodka.

Sherrie admitted she often blacked out or felt ill. And after four years, she finally conceded she needed help.

She was sent on a three-week course to the School of Urban Wilderness Survival in North Carolina. And she so impressed organisers that on completion they gave her a scholarship to a top US boarding school.

Sherrie, from Northampton – who now insists she is only a "moderate social drinker" – confessed: "I drank more than anyone else. I was a drunken teenager."

Months after she began drinking, the youngster stopped going to school. And by 14 her boozing was causing such chaos at home that her mum threw her out.

Even then, Sherrie continued to go to bars which offered "all you can drink for £13" while she lived with her grandparents and friends.

She spent £28 of her £45 income support on drink.

Sherrie said she first got drunk after downing alcopops at a nightclub – dressed in her school uniform.

She said: "It got to the point I was drinking every day. When I went out I'd start with Stella, share a bottle of Vodka and a bottle of Archers schnapps then go out for more. I'd have a shot after every half of lager.

"I was really bad. I didn't realise I was an alcoholic till I went to America and looked back at my life. It was a waste of my life but I have a better adult life now.

"I want to do more with it. I've wasted two years of my life clubbing – I'm already bored of it and I'm only 16.

"This experience has taught me to appreciate things and realise there are other ways of doing and acting on things. I'm not going to go back to that ever."

During her US course, Sherrie was forced to trek through mountains with no access to drink, cigarettes, drugs, friends or family.

She carried a tent, food rations and clothes and spent two nights in isolation, setting up her own camp, lighting fires and cooking.

Sherrie saw a counsellor and at last began to realise what she was doing to herself.

She now has her own flat and works in a call centre. She is due to start at the Massachusetts boarding school next month.

Mum Linda, 42, said the course was "the best thing that could ever have happened to her."

Linda told how Sherrie's boozing left the family on a knife edge. She said: "It was pretty frightening. I had to protect my other children. Sherrie became extremely violent. She never went to school and came home drunk. She would come in, thumping the doors, thumping the walls, smashing things and breaking things.

"Then she's start shouting at her siblings. It was unbearable."

Sun GP Carol Cooper said she had never heard of a youngster drinking so much.

She said: "This girl was clearly an alcoholic at 12. Young people get drunk more easily because their livers aren't as mature.

"They are therefore more likely to pass out or go into a coma. Sometimes the first symptom is coma or even death."

Anna Pelly, assistant producer of the TV show, said Sherrie had beaten her drink demons. She said: "She's got a promising future. We are all really pleased."

© The Sun

NEWSPAPER ARTICLES TO GET TEENAGERS TALKING — Food and health

Glossary

1 binge drinking: drinking a lot of alcohol very quickly
2 booze: (noun) alcohol; (verb) to drink alcohol
3 to sink (colloquial): to drink large amounts of
4 hooked on: addicted to
5 alcopops: a sweet alcoholic drink
6 a pint: 0.568 of a litre
7 a shot: a small amount of (vodka, whisky etc.)
8 blacked out: passed out, fainted
9 income support: government money paid to those on low incomes
10 downing (colloquial): drinking a lot quickly
11 on a knife edge: in real danger, at risk
12 a GP: a General Practitioner, a family doctor
13 pass out: faint

2 As you read, match the words from the article 1–9 with their meanings a–i.

1 pals   a) a free place at
2 steadily   b) fainted, lost consciousness
3 intake   c) told her to leave
4 blacked out   d) banging, hitting really hard
5 conceded   e) friends
6 a scholarship to   f) long, hard journey
7 threw her out   g) admitted, accepted
8 trek   h) more and more, increasingly
9 thumping   i) consumption, how much you drink

3 Complete the journalist's notes about Sherrie's story.

Background
a A typical night's drinking would be vodka, 11 _____ and 4½ half pints of _____
b When Sherrie came home drunk, she would thump the _____ and _____, smash things and _____ at family.

Effects of drinking
c Stella would _____ out or feel ill. She was often found in a _____ stupor.

The cure
d Stella was sent on a _____-week course at the School of Urban Wilderness _____ in North Carolina.
e The course involved _____ through mountains with no access to _____, _____ or drink and no contact with _____ and family.
f She spent _____ nights alone setting up her _____, lighting fires and cooking the _____ she took with her.

Today
g Stella now works in a _____ and has her own _____. She's won a scholarship to a top boarding _____ in _____.

4 Now discuss the following.

a What do you think of the Sherrie Cooke story? Do you admire her or feel sorry for her?
b What did Sherrie learn from those four years of drinking?
c Some British councils ban the drinking of alcohol in public places like market squares and parks. Is that a good idea? Why/Why not?
d When is it acceptable/unacceptable to drink? Should people be allowed to drink alcohol:
   before they drive a car? on television? at football matches? at school? in restaurants?
e What effect does alcohol have? Is it something that helps people relax and enjoy themselves, or is it a dangerous thing that causes anti-social behaviour?

5 A company called Superpubs wants to open a new pub in your area and they have applied to the local council for permission.

The Superpub would have five bars and seats for 1,000 people. It would create 120 new jobs and stay open until late at night. The local council are holding a public meeting before coming to a decision.

a Divide into four groups, then write and role play the arguments put forward by one of the following. Use the language below.
   Group one: the managing director of the brewery.
   Group two: the police.
   Group three: local residents in favour of the proposal.
   Group four: local residents against the proposal.

Group 1
One of our Superpubs would be great for this area because _____

Group 2
As far as the police are concerned, there are a number of things to consider. For example, _____

Group 3
My name is _____ and I'm a local resident. I'm for the plan because I'm worried about _____

Group 4
My name is _____. I'm against the plan as for me, _____

b After all the different views have been presented, take a class vote. Would you give permission for a Superpub in your area?

29 Opportunities for wealth

On this and the following pages are two articles about countries struggling against poverty. The tiny islands of São Tomé and Principe lie 400 kilometres off the west coast of Gabon. Until recently, their 140,000 inhabitants were among the poorest people in the world. Then, in 2004, scientists made an incredible discovery. Under the ocean around the islands they found oil worth $50,000,000,000, enough money to make everyone in this former Portuguese colony a dollar millionaire. This article tells the story of how oil may be about to transform the lives of the people on the islands.

Chocolate isles struggle to avert the 'curse' of oil

BY TIM BUTCHER IN SÃO TOMÉ

OFF the West African coast, the sharks are circling the sleeping "chocolate islands" of São Tomé and Principe, eager to bite of slices of billions of pounds of hoped-for oil revenues.

One of Africa's poorest nations is being spoken of as a new Kuwait following recent surveys showing that up to 11 billion barrels of oil lie under its territorial waters.

Prospects of an oil boom in the tiny former Portuguese colony have attracted a wave of charlatans and swindlers and São Tomé is keen to avoid becoming the next African country to prove that oil can be more of a curse than a blessing.

Many of the people of Nigeria, Angola, Equatorial Guinea and elsewhere grew poorer as vast oil revenues were stolen by corrupt regimes and businessmen – a situation that São Tomé's chubby and affable leader, President Fradique de Menezes, says he wants to prevent.

Oil has already led to unrest. It was said to have help foment an attempted coup last July, when a group of disaffected soldiers temporarily seized power from Mr de Menezes.

He survived and has made progress. He has followed the advice of western economists about how to develop the oil sector, and has presided over a bidding round among oil companies that is seen as the most transparent in African oil industry history.

"This place really is on the up more than it ever has been, but the sharks are already circling in the water," said the former cocoa trader.

Every few days, charter planes full of businessmen from Nigeria, Angola and elsewhere fly into São Tomé's tiny international airport where the grass grows waist high on either side of the runway.

São Tomé, with a population of only 140,000, is also being wooed by the United States, which had deployed a military liaison officer there as part of its war on terrorism.

In military terms, the country is virtually helpless, with no aircraft or tanks. Its only working naval boat, a small coastguard launch, was recently stolen and ended up in Nigeria.

Until recently, many British diplomats would have struggled to find the islands on a map, but London is now increasing aid money, with £135,000 going to fund a project of public education about how to use oil revenues.

For now, São Tomé's government appears clean, but it also seems somewhat out of its depth and was forced to renegotiate ill-conceived contracts for lucrative prospecting rights owned by a rich Nigerian businessman.

With oil revenues still years away, the country owes £200 million in foreign debt – one of the highest per capita levels in Africa – and remains seriously under-developed.

Out on the *rocas*, the Portuguese-built cocoa plantations – now in decline – thousands live in poverty. High humidity and temperatures have rotted the once-grand plantation houses, and a tangle of jungle has smothered the once well-ordered cocoa fields.

Poverty remains rife for most São Toméans. Cocoa growing might have earned the place the soubriquet of "chocolate islands" as Portugal profited during the colonial era, but it now generates only £3 million in exports.

The rest of the £30 million national budget comes from foreign aid. This seems likely to be dwarfed by oil revenues. The rights to explore just one block of seabed will earn São Tomé £50 million later this year from Chevron-Texaco and there are plenty more blocks up for tender.

"If you have high poverty, high expectations of oil revenues and a low level of capacity to deliver, you might have a bomb on your hands" said Rafael Branco, the suave former oil minister.

"The challenge is to defuse that bomb."

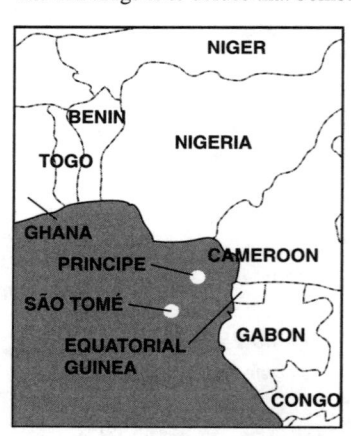

© The Daily Telegraph

NEWSPAPER ARTICLES TO GET TEENAGERS TALKING World issues

1) Before you read, discuss the following.
What do you think happened after the oil was discovered?
Who do you think will get all the money?
Who will lose out?

Glossary

1 *charlatans and swindlers*: dishonest people who cheat you out of your money
2 *foment*: encourage or cause something bad
3 *sobriquet*: nickname
4 *a bidding round*: when different international companies bid for something
5 *prospecting rights*: a contract that allows you to look for oil or minerals
6 *up for tender*: available to the highest bidder

2) As you read, answer the questions to find the meaning to these words.

a If you *avert* something, do you make it happen or stop it happening?
b Is a *boom* a period of growth or decline?
c Is a *swindler* honest or dishonest?
d Is an *affable* person friendly or unfriendly?
e If you are *disaffected*, are you happy or unhappy?
f If you are *out of your depth*, do you know what you are doing or not?
g Is a *lucrative* business profitable or unprofitable?
h Which is bigger, a *plant* or a *plantation*?
i If a bomb is *defused*, is it safe or unsafe?

3) Now complete the notes with information from the article.

The islands of São Tomé and Principe

Location: 400 kms west of Gabon

Size: 5 kms by 7 kms

Estimated oil reserves: (a) _____ barrels

Airport: tiny, waist-high grass either side of the (b) _____

Population: (c) _____

Number of military aircraft: (d) _____

Number of tanks: (e) _____

Outstanding debts of: (f) _____

Main crop grown on the plantations: (g) _____

Annual exports worth: (h) _____

Chevron-Texaco will pay (i) _____ to explore one block of the seabed

Now read an appeal by Nelson Mandela. ➡

WHAT A DIFFERENCE A DAY MAKES

A LETTER TO YOU – FROM NELSON MANDELA

Dear Mirror readers

Today we live in a world that remains divided. A world in which we have made great progress and advances in science and technology.

But it is also a world where millions of children die because they have no access to medicines.

We live in a world where knowledge and information have made enormous strides, yet millions of children are not in school.

We live in a world where the AIDS 2 pandemic threatens the very fabric of our lives. Yet we spend more money on weapons than on ensuring treatment and support for the millions infected by HIV. It is a world of great promise and hope. It is also a world of despair, disease and hunger.

Millions of people in the world's poorest countries are trapped in the prison of poverty.

It is time to set them free.

Poverty is not natural, it is man-made and can be overcome by the action of human beings.

The leaders of the world's richest countries have already promised to focus on the issue of poverty, especially in Africa.

The steps they must take to bring this about are very clear and the first is ensuring trade justice.

The second is an end to the debt crisis for the poorest countries.

The third is to deliver much more aid and to make sure it is of the highest quality.

I say to all those leaders – do not look the other way, do not hesitate. Recognise that the world is hungry for actions, not words.

You too have the opportunity to tell them that they must act with courage and vision.

Sometimes it falls upon a generation to be great.

You can be that great generation.

© Daily Mirror

NEWSPAPER ARTICLES TO GET TEENAGERS TALKING World issues

In 2005, the leaders of the world's richest countries travelled to Scotland to talk about the problems of world poverty and international debt. There were two big questions at the meeting: Should rich nations cancel the debts of the poorest countries, and should they also spend more on aid? A campaign group called 'Make Poverty History' had no doubts. For them, the answers were 'yes' and 'yes' and they organised a series of concerts (known as Live8) to drive their message home. As three billion people watched these concerts live on TV, Nelson Mandela, the former President of South Africa, explained why these issues effect us all.

4 **Before you read, discuss the following.**
What do you know about Nelson Mandela? What role did he play in the fight against apartheid?

5 **As you read, match the words from the article 1–10 with their meanings a–j.**

1 divided	a) release/liberate (them)
2 have no access to	b) make (this) happen
3 strides	c) defeated, beaten
4 set (them) free	d) (you) have the responsibility to
5 overcome	e) guaranteeing
6 issue	f) ignore the problem
7 bring (this) about	g) can't have, can't get
8 ensuring	h) steps forward, progress
9 look the other way	i) question, subject, problem
10 it falls upon (you) to	j) separated

6 **Complete the journalist's notes with information from the text.**

Mandela says ...
The world has made great progress in (a) _____, technology, (b) _____ and information.
But, millions of children die because they can't get (c) _____ and millions of children don't go to (d) _____
We spend more money on (e) _____ than on tackling the (f) _____ crisis.
Poverty is not natural, it is (g) _____-made.
Things that must be done ...
• ensure trade justice and get rid of the (h) _____ of the poorest countries
• deliver more high-quality (i) _____
• the leaders of the world should not (j) _____ the other way
• the world wants (k) _____ not words

Glossary

1 strides: big steps, great progress
2 pandemic: an infection that spreads across the world
3 threatens the very fabric of: puts the most important things in danger
4 HIV (human immunodeficiency virus): the AIDS virus

7 **Read the Fact file and discuss the following questions.**

a) Why is oil so important?
b) Some people say that modern wars are often fought because of oil. Do you agree?
c) By 2015, Africa will be producing more oil than the Middle East. How will that change the world?

Fact file

- In 2005, the year of Live 8, the oil company BP made £100 profit every second.
- Tax revenues from oil pay for more than half of Britain's national health service.
- A fifth of the world's population live on less than a dollar a day.
- There are 18 countries in Africa that were poorer in 2005 than they were in 1985.
- It is estimated that a third of all international aid goes 'missing' through corruption.
- A billion people are illiterate.
- A billion children live in poverty.
- If you add together the money of the three richest people in the world, the figure is higher than the combined annual income of the world's 48 poorest countries.
- It would cost 1% of what we spend on weapons to put every child into school.

8 **Now decide how the world can best help poor countries.**

a Get into four groups. Each group chooses one of the ways suggested below and decides why it is the best way to help.
 • Give more aid.
 • Cancel the poor countries' debts.
 • Have fairer rules for trade.
 • Do not interfere and leave the countries alone.
b Now each group tells the class why their way is the best.
c Have a class vote on the best way.

30 The old soldiers

In 1944, during the Second World War, there was a major battle on the rough beaches of Normandy, in north west France. The fighting began on 6th June (now known as D-Day) when a wave of ships launched from Britain brought thousands of soldiers towards the German guns. Many soldiers died seconds after landing on the beach. The event was commemorated sixty years later with presidents and royalty giving formal speeches. The most remarkable images were of the old soldiers, now in their 70s and 80s, returning to the places where many of their colleagues fell. In this article, The Times followed five British veterans on their journey back.

1 Before you read, discuss the following.
What do you think the presidents, prime ministers, royalty and generals said at the official ceremony?

Glossary

1 veterans: old soldiers
2 South Lancashire Regiment: a division of the British Army
3 chummy: friendly
4 stormed: rushed
5 88mm: an 88mm gun
6 rheumy: watery
7 the high and mighty: important people (VIPs)
8 hurrah: celebration
9 the Somme: the location of a major battle in the First World War
10 the Prince of Wales: Prince Charles, the future king of England
11 throng: fill

2 As you read, answer the questions to find the meaning of these words.
a If a memory *fades*, does it get stronger or weaker?
b Is a *placid* sea rough or calm?
c If you *wade* through the sea, is the water up to your ankles or up to your waist?
d Is *dusk* at the same time as sunrise or sunset?
e Is a *telling observation* interesting or uninteresting?
f Are *adversaries* enemies or friends?
g If the event is *poignant*, will it be happy or sad?
h Does a *host of* mean many or few?
i If you are *in the limelight*, are people watching you or ignoring you?
j If you act *with discretion*, are you careful or careless?

3 Now circle T (True) or F (False).
a Sword Beach was full of people yesterday. T/F
b Reg and his friends landed on the beach late in the afternoon. T/F
c They have clear memories of that day. T/F
d It took them about two hours to capture Hermanville-sur-Mer. T/F
e More than half of their company were killed. T/F
f The five soldiers swam ashore. T/F
g The ceremony to remember their colleagues will be held at dusk. T/F
h The Prince of Wales says we should now forget the soldiers. T/F
i Thousands of veterans will parade through the village of Arromaches. T/F
j The leader of Germany will attend the commemoration service. T/F

4 Now discuss the following.
a Why do countries go to war?
b What do wars achieve? Who loses?
c Would you fight in a war if the government told you to?
d Are there ideas or philosophies worth dying for?
e Is there a difference between war and terrorism?
f Why is there so much violence in the world?
g Many children like to pretend to be soliders. Why? Do people enjoy fighting?

5 Imagine you were one of the soldiers on their way to Normandy in 1944. In groups, write the conversation you imagine took place between Reg and his four friends.
a Give your characters a range of feelings: one may be terrified, one excited, another proud to be fighting for his country, etc.
b Start the conversation when the boat is 300 metres off the coast. End it when their boat arrives at the beaches of Normandy.
c Act out the dialogue for the rest of the class.

Alan Hamilton joins veterans of the South Lancashire Regiment on their return to Normandy

Princes and politicians will invade Normandy this weekend but yesterday, on a deserted stretch of Sword Beach, the day belonged to Reg Timberlake and his old comrades of the South Lancashire Regiment.

They stood, jovial and chummy old men, at the exact spot where they had stormed ashore in the early hours of June 6, 1944.

Their memories have faded into a hazy recollection of barbed wire, murderous 88mm enemy fire and skies black with smoke. At moments like that, the mind is too engaged otherwise to film the fine detail for posterity.

This was Sword Beach White and their objective was to capture the village of Hermanville-sur-Mer. They had done so in little more than two hours, but at great cost. Their company of 200 sustained 11 officer casualties and 98 other ranks; their commanding officer, Lieutenant-Colonel Richard Burberry, was killed by a sniper within minutes of landing.

Yesterday the tide was in, the sea placid and the afternoon muggy. Reg, 82, and his mates John, Norman, Vince and Tommy, gazed with rheumy eyes on an empty sea and recalled how they had waded ashore from the greatest armada ever assembled. But veterans do not talk of armadas or wider pictures; for every man on the ground, war was a personal battle to kill and survive.

They will return to Hermanville tomorrow night, when the high and mighty have departed. Those that are still able will march to the village war cemetery and, in the quiet of dusk, hold their own remembrance service by the graves of their comrades.

More than 10,000 British veterans alone will be here by tonight, not to mention American and Canadian contingents, all celebrating their last great communal hurrah.

Of the two million men who took part in three months of fighting to liberate Normandy, on some days with a casualty rate as high as at the Somme, only 175,000 landed on that first day. But every man who fought in that campaign basks in the glory of that first wave of invasion in the early hours of June 6 which turned the tide of the Second World War.

No one is more aware of the effort and sacrifice than the Prince of Wales, who is the principal attraction at a series of commemorative events in Normandy today. In a D-Day message released yesterday, he made an especially telling observation.

"Above all, we should recall that so many of those who died were of the same age as both my sons are today. It is only that way we can begin to understand the real extent of the sacrifice that was made, and the heartrending suffering of the families in this country and in France whose loved ones were torn away from them in the course of doing their duty."

We must never forget that victory did not come without enormous cost, the Prince said. "Sixty years later, with old adversaries now reconciled, together enjoying peace, prosperity and better common understanding, it is hard to imagine the devastation wrought on France."

The Prince concluded: "We owe these men and women our profound respect and everlasting prayers of gratitude."

Officials expect nearly 7,000 British veterans to attend the commemoration of the first invasion. Even greater numbers are expected at the principal British events tomorrow, which the Queen will attend.

More than 10,000 will fill the war cemetery at Bayeux for a major Anglo-French commemoration service, and 11,500 will join perhaps the most poignant spectacle of all, the last great parade of British veterans through the seaside village of Arromanches, where the miraculous Mulberry Harbour, which landed millions of tons of supplies, still pokes its decaying concrete shoulders above the waves.

The Queen, presidents Chirac, Bush and Putin, Tony Blair and a host of European monarchs and Commonwealth prime ministers will briefly seize the limelight tomorrow afternoon for an international ceremony. For the first time the German Chancellor will join the line-up of dignitaries; small knots of Germans who fought in the war have been visiting Normandy in recent weeks, but with discretion and in small numbers.

Some British veterans have been angered by the bureaucracy, form-filling and restrictions which have interfered with their wish to attend certain set-piece events. But the ceremonies take place against the background of a new kind of war, and a heavy French and American anti-terrorist presence is plainly visible on the ground and in the air.

But nothing has prevented Reg Timberlake and thousands like him from having their own private commemorations of thanks for the comradeship of those who survived, and of respectful memory for the legions who did not.

© The Times

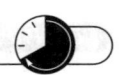

NEWSPAPER ARTICLES TO GET TEENAGERS TALKING — World issues

31 Global warming

Environmental groups like Greenpeace say the world is getting hotter every year as greenhouse gases punch a huge hole in the ozone layer which protects us from the heat of the sun. In countries like Zambia, this rise in temperature can mean the difference between life and death as the dry earth makes it impossible for farmers to grow enough crops to survive. No one knows this better than Julius Njame and the villagers of Chickani who see their farms hit by drought and their wells running dry.

1) Before you read, discuss the following.
Some scientists say that global warming is disrupting the weather and causing drought, flooding, hurricanes etc. What types of extreme weather have been in the news recently? Describe what happened and how people were effected.

Glossary
1 on hold: paused, stuck, unable to move forward
2 on the front line: leading the fight, most effected by
3 is in for a rough ride: is going to have a difficult time
4 subsistence farmers: farmers who can only grow enough to feed themselves

2) As you read, answer the questions to find the meaning of these words.
a When people *murmur*, do they make a loud sound or a soft sound?
b If you give your *assent*, do you agree or disagree?
c If crops *wilt*, do they get stonger or weaker?
d If you *hang on*, do you keep going or give up?
e Would a *perilous* situation be safe or very dangerous?
f When the wells *run dry*, are they full or empty?
g Is a *vast* area huge or tiny?
h Does a *meteorologist* study the weather or how to grow crops?
i If you are *destitute*, are you extremely rich or extremely poor?
j If a river *dries up*, is it full or empty?

3) Choose the best answer.
a In Chikani last year...
   (1) there were heavy rains in November.
   (2) it rained for three weeks in December.
   (3) the first rains came a month later than normal.
b The villagers ...
   (1) agree with what Julius says.
   (2) have not harvested any maize this year.
   (3) have rice as their staple diet.
c Global warming will ...
   (1) make summers colder.
   (2) make growing seasons longer.
   (3) make sea levels fall.
d In southern Africa ...
   (1) they have had extremes of weather for a long time.
   (2) the climate is becoming more predictable.
   (3) severe weather is becoming less frequent.

4) Now discuss the following.
a Does global warming affect us all, or just people in Africa? What would happen if the ice caps melted?
b How are these things affected by global warming?

the rainforests	wild animals	pollution
disease	water levels	water supplies
political relations between countries		

c What practical things could be done to reduce the effects of global warming?
d Many people do not care about global warming. Why is this? Do you care?

5) Your group have been asked to take part in a radio programme called *Eight degrees more* about the effects of global warming. The programme will look at how the world would change if temperatures rose by another eight degrees celsius. Discuss the following.

a What would happen in your part of the world if the spring, summer, autumn and winter were all eight degrees warmer?
b Would it be a good thing or a bad thing?
c Write your ideas. Use the following language.

If this country was eight degrees hotter than it is now, there would be all sorts of changes. For example, it would be ...
People would feel ... and animals would ...
The cities would be ... and the countryside ...
All the seasons would be different. For example ...
On the one hand, there would be good things, like ...
But there would also be some problems, for example ...
Overall, we think an increase of eight degrees all year round would ...

d Now present your predictions to the rest of the class. Does everyone agree?

IN THE LAND WHERE LIFE IS ON HOLD

Africa is on the front line of climate change reports John Vidal. And floods, drought and famine show the continent is in for a rough ride

Thirty men and 22 women sit beneath a great mugamba tree on the edge of Chikani village in southern Zambia. "This is what happened," says Julius Njame, standing and speaking formally. "We prepared our fields for planting seeds in the November rains. We waited but the first drop didn't fall till December 20. After a day, the rains stopped. Three weeks later, it started to rain again. But then it stopped again after a few days. Since then, we have had no rain."

The crowd murmurs its assent and one by one, people stand to tell how their own crops wilted and how little they have harvested this year. Anderson says he got five bags of the staple maize crop, Lovewell eight, Jennifer two, Felice three and Jonah seven. Some say they have lost almost everything and will be eating wild foods within weeks. Most say they will be able to hang on only until next month.

The people of Chikani are experiencing a climatic phenomenon taking place around the world. But the effect of global warming on a village of central African subsistence farmers is different and far more serious than on America or Europe.

Some northerners bask in the idea that global warming promises delightful summers and longer growing seasons. But rising sea levels and future climatic extremes, causing even a small change in rainfall patterns or temperatures, is perilous now for vast areas of Africa.

Where the rich northern city or farmer can adapt, the families of millions of poor Zambian, Congolese or Malawian farmers go hungry for months; urban water supplies are interrupted and wells run dry.

Africa is in the frontline of climate change, and for the people of Chikani it makes the difference between food and hunger, migration and stability, sufficiency and destitution - even life and death.

Droughts, floods, unseasonal rains, extreme weather and natural disasters have long been common in southern Africa, but new studies are finding a pattern of increasing climatic variability and unpredictability. According to UN agencies and national meteorologists, severe dry and wet periods have become more frequent in the past two to three decades.

Old Jonah in Chikani, who has 24 children from three wives, doesn't need academics to tell him the climate is changing. "These are the worst rains ever," he says. "The pattern of rainfall is definitely changing. I remember many bad years but this is the first time the river Musaya has ever dried up. This is the first time that we have only had one place to find water."

Crop failure this year extends across swathes of southern Zambia, northern Zimbabawe and Malawi. According to the UN's food organisation, 20 countries in Africa are this month facing food emergencies following droughts or "adverse" weather.

© The Guardian

32 Chemical alert

In November 2005, an 11-year-old schoolgirl called Mollie Clements was invited to speak at the European Parliament in Strasbourg. Mollie had just taken part in a research programme that revealed she had 75 man-made chemicals in her blood and she asked the politicians to do something to make the environment cleaner and healthier. Incredibly, just a few hours after Mollie's speech, the European Parliament did what she asked, banning some toxins and forcing companies to do more tests on the chemicals they use.

1 Before you read, discuss the following.

Are you surprised that an 11-year-old would have 75 man-made chemicals in her blood?
Where do you think those chemicals came from?

Glossary

1 WWF: World Wildlife Fund, an environmental charity
2 a battery of tests: a wide range of tests; all sorts of tests
3 scores of: many (a score is 20)
4 PVC: polyvinyl chloride, a plastic material found in clothing and floor coverings

2 As you read, match the words from the article 1-10 with their meanings a-j.

1 jolly   a) all over, throughout
2 up and down   b) a warning
3 contaminated   c) hard, strict, very detailed
4 hazardous   d) happy
5 rigorous   e) in fact
6 banned   f) during
7 actually   g) forbidden, not allowed
8 toxins   h) dangerous
9 in the course of   i) poisoned
10 a wake-up call   j) poisons

3 Now choose the best answer.

a The survey showed that ...
  (1) all the Clements family have at least 25 chemicals in their blood.
  (2) Mollie's grandmother has 75 chemicals in her blood.
  (3) children have fewer chemicals in their blood than older people.

b The WWF study ...
  (1) tested nine different families.
  (2) tested Mollie's great grandparents.
  (3) tested for 104 man-made chemicals.
c Scientists ...
  (1) understand the long-term effects of these chemicals.
  (2) expected children to have fewer chemicals than their grandparents.
  (3) have no idea how chemicals are passed from one generation to the next.
d You can reduce the harmful chemicals in your blood by ...
  (1) dry cleaning all your clothes.
  (2) eating more dairy food.
  (3) ventilating the rooms you live and work in.

4 Now discuss the following.

a Should we ban all man-made chemicals from household products and food?
b Are you worried by the findings of the WWF report, or do you think it is all scaremongering, a fuss about nothing?
c Do people worry too much about such reports? Should we all just live for today and take life as it comes?
d Should we test man-made chemicals on animals to see if they are safe for humans?

5 You are an environmental group and have been given a large amount of money to campaign on a particular issue. Divide into seven groups representing one of the following campaigns.

- ban smoking in all public places
- encourage people to drive electric cars
- stop flying
- close down factories that cause pollution
- recycle more
- forbid the use of pesticides
- prohibit plastics and only use wood and natural products

a In your groups, think of arguments to explain why your campaign is the best way to spend the money.
b Present your arguments to the rest of the class.
c Have a vote on the best way to spend the money.

THE 75 TOXIC CHEMICALS IN OUR BLOOD

by Rachel Murphy

THEY are an ordinary hard-working British family with three happy children and a jolly granny.

Lined up outside their Devon home, the Clements are typical of a million other mums, dads, teenagers, kids and pensioners up and down the country. But behind their smiles lies a shocking reality.

Each member of the family has been contaminated with more than 25 hazardous, man-made chemicals which could be slowly destroying their health.

And the rest of us are likely to have similar levels of chemicals in our blood.

Mum Sara, dad Ian, their children Louis, Amy, and Mollie, and grandmother Patricia Humphries all took part in a WWF study of seven families to find out how polluted our bodies are.

It is the first time that three generations of the same family have been subjected to such a rigorous battery of tests for a total of 104 man-made chemicals.

It was thought that grandparents - having been exposed to chemicals that are now banned and with many more years of exposure behind them - might have been more contaminated than the younger generations.

But the children were actually found to have 75 different chemicals in their blood compared to the 56 in their grandparents' blood.

Many of the chemicals are used in the manufacture of furniture, TVs, non-stick pans, carpets and clothing.

Experts believe the children may have inherited older toxins from their mother's blood in pregnancy or through breast milk, as well as being bombarded by scores of newer chemicals in the course of their daily lives.

Many are so new that scientists have no idea how they will react with older chemicals already in the body - and we don't know what the long term effect on health will be.

"This is a wake-up call to the UK government and the European Union to stop repeating the mistakes of the past and ensure these chemicals are banned and replaced with safer alternatives," says Justin Woolford, WWF Chemicals and Health campaign director.

FACT FILE
For more information about the WWF campaign, go to their website at www.wwf.org.uk.

---

10 ways to reduce these toxins in your blood:
1. Eat more organic food.
2. Cut your intake of dairy products and red meat.
3. Don't use pesticides in the garden.
4. Avoid dry cleaning.
5. Choose natural fibres for soft furnishings, wood floors or tiles.
6. Ventilate your home and office well.
7. Don't let children chew soft plastic toys.
8. Avoid PVC flooring.
9. Avoid anything treated with non-stick chemicals.
10. Use natural soaps and cleaning products.

© The Daily Mirror

ANSWERS

1 How often do you touch people?

Exercise 2

Across
4 triggers 5 flow 6 tighten 8 stiffen 9 routine
10 spontaneously 11 acquaintances
Down
1 irritates 2 frown 3 clues 6 touchy 7 handshake

Exercise 3
a3 b1 c3 d3 e2

2 You are what you drink

Exercise 2
1f 2h 3g 4i 5a 6b 7c 8e 9d

Exercise 3
1 cappucino 2 decaf 3 filter 4 instant 5 latte
6 espresso 7 frappucino 8 decaf 9 filter 10 cafetiere
11 black coffee 12 cappucino

3 Things you love the most

Exercise 2
a selfish b the daughter of your brother or sister
c the son of your brother or sister d visible
e embarrassed f unselfish g more and more
h friendship i value j difficult to understand

Exercise 3
a1 b2 c3 d2

4 Going bananas

Exercise 2
1e 2f 3a 4b 5i 6c 7d 8g 9h

Exercise 3
a true b false c false d false e false f false
g true h false i false j true

5 Too much TV?

Exercise 2
a limit b too kind c finishes d using your finger
e takes away f teaches g exchange h work together
i shouting j brothers and sisters

Exercise 3
a true b false c true d true e true f true g false
h false i false j true k true l true

6 Shopping with Big Brother

Exercise 2
a start b connected to c you take them to court
d you copy someone else e inside f follow
g negatively h wear i collect j advanced

Exercise 3
a2 b1 c1 d3 e2 f1

7 The computer games addict

Exercise 2
1c 2f 3g 4a 5b 6d 7e

Exercise 3
a2 b1 c1 d3 e3

8 Glasses for your dog

Exercise 2
1 sense 2 pupil 3 vet 4 colours 5 sight 6 bark 7 canine
8 headlights 9 retina 10 ensure
Hidden word: spectacles

Exercise 3
a true b false c true d true e false f true g false
h true i false

Exercise 4
a Love me, love my dog. b It's raining cats and dogs.
c Let sleeping dogs lie. d You can't teach an old dog
new tricks. e It's a dog's life. f Every dog has its day.
g A dog is a man's best friend.

9 Helping the homeless

Exercise 2
1f 2d 3e 4j 5g 6b 7c 8i 9a 10h

Exercise 3
a false b false c true d true e true f true g false
h true i false j true

Exercise 5
1d 2i 3g 4a 5h 6c 7j 8b 9e 10f

Exercise 6
a pregnant b old rugs/plastic c water
d soup/bread rolls e food f begging g commuters
h drugs/alcohol i respect j flat

10 Compensation culture

Exercise 2

Across
1 crippled 4 spokeswoman 5 vet 7 awkwardly 8 bright 9 grabbing 10 motionless
Down
2 leapt 3 spine 6 heartbreaking

Exercise 3

a true b false c true d false e false f false g false h false i false j false

Exercise 4

a climbed b very quickly c plants/small trees d coming to an agreement e bought f went quickly g a kind of book h someone who enjoys sweet things

Exercise 5

a 3, 5 b 2, 5 c 7 d 1, 4, 7 e 2, 6 f 4 g 7, 8 h 6

11 Free money

Exercise 2

1d 2h 3e 4f 5c 6a 7b

Exercise 3

a true b true c true d false e false f true g false h false i false

12 Starting again

Exercise 2

a very short b starting c in prison d lucky e getting into trouble f drinking heavily g increased quickly h well respected i appeared j admit the truth

Exercise 3

a false b false c true d true e false f true g true h true i false j true k true l false

13 Money matters

Exercise 2

a give it b almost all c many d abandoning e thinking about f a share in the company g supporter h having no real direction i joined j released

Exercise 3

a cars b baseball c Catholic d swapped (exchanged) e Michigan f 900 g 6,100 h foster/orphanage i Marine Corps j abortion

Exercise 4

a Money doesn't grow on trees. b Time is money. c Money can't buy you love. d Money talks. e A fool and his money are soon parted. f Money makes the world go round. (This saying is a variation on the old proverb *Love makes the world go round*.)

Exercise 6

1i 2j 3a 4g 5b 6c 7h 8d 9e 10f

Exercise 7

a luxury (expensive, beloved)/£74,285 b 24 c English d alarmed e phone/cleaning/security f birthday g ship h movie (film) i photographers j suites

Exercise 8

1 Monaghan 2 both (Tom Monaghan's brother got a Volkswagen Beetle for his half share) 3 Monaghan 4 both 5 Monaghan 6 Beckham

14 Charities

Exercise 2

a hoover b kite c vending d weaved e surf f bargain g bid h nip

Exercise 3

a go for a long drive/weave through a crowd/whizz around the supermarket/nip across the road and back/ride a bicycle/explore somewhere by train
b surf the internet
c fly a kite/take a frisbee to the park/ride a bicycle/ (perhaps also enjoy an exhibition and prune your prize roses)
d go out bargain hunting/whizz around the supermarket/bid at an auction/use a vending machine
e decorate a room/change a light bulb/re-wire a plug/put up shelving/re-arrange your living room
f fill out a lottery ticket/play bingo
g whizz around a supermarket/light a barbecue/follow a recipe
h prune your prize roses
i read your children a story/surf the internet/follow a recipe/curl up with a good book
j decide on a new hairstyle/put on a bit of make-up

15 Disciplining children

Exercise 2

1h 2d 3g 4a 5f 6b 7c 8e

Exercise 3

a Alice b Claire (but perhaps also Alice who wouldn't hit an older child) c Alice d Claire e Claire f both g Claire h Alice i Claire j Alice

16 International companies

Exercise 2

a probably b many c moving d light rain e connected to f absolutely perfect g filled with h rising and falling i difficult j hired k solves problems l growing fast

Exercise 3

a directory enquiries b five and a half c steak and kidney d 2,000 e well f soap g aliases h employees/branches i trendy j weather/pets

Exercise 5

a Nike b Starbucks, Yahoo c Aston Martin, Nokia, Haribo, IKEA d Ebay, Toyota, Pepsi e Mitsubishi f Google g Coca-Cola h Pepsi i Adidas j Tesco k Lycos l Lego (and perhaps IKEA)

17 From teacher to plumber

Exercise 2

Across
2 suit 3 chatting 4 fitting 5 gobsmacking 9 boffin 11 boiler 13 amazing
Down
1 quitting 6 skint 7 double 8 salary 10 brainbox 12 research

Exercise 3

a 23,000/10,000 b strike c boarding house d joining e boiler f gobsmacked g contract h education i course j up to

18 Does punctuation matter?

Exercise 2

1 stall 2 abbreviate 3 marrow 4 window 5 research 6 pound 7 littered 8 point 9 commonplace
Hidden word: semicolon

Exercise 3

1c 2e 3d 4f 5b 6a

Exercise 6

a David thought Caroline looked really tired.
(= Caroline looks tired)
David, thought Caroline, looked really tired.
(= David looks tired)
b A woman without her man is nothing.
(= a woman needs a man)
A woman: without her, man is nothing.
(= a man needs a woman)
c The girls who had finished the exam left the room.
(= some of them left)
The girls, who had finished the exam, left the room.
(= all of them left)

19 Does prison work?

Exercise 2

1g 2e 3a 4c 5f 6i 7h 8j 9d 10b

Exercise 3

a true b false c false d false e true f false g false h true i true j true

20 The island doctor

Exercise 2

1f 2d 3e 4c 5g 6i 7h 8a 9b

Exercise 3

a no/3 b year/doctor (GP)/advertisement (ad, advert)/inundated (flooded/swamped) c bungalow/sea d 1,500 e 60/3 f ferry g deer/salmon/sand/whisky h instruments i aunt j ambulance

21 A man's job?

Exercise 2

a abandon b reject them c try your hardest d ten years e oar f hit it g they get on well h reject i difficult j protect

Exercise 3

a false b false c false (two women and four men) d false e true f false g true h false i false j false k true

22 The school day

Exercise 2

a moves slowly b falling slowly c writes quickly and not very neatly d forbid e reach the same standard as f sacrifice g deep-rooted h forget about i too serious j wealth

Exercise 3

a 80 b 5/4 c 10 d fourth e natural f second g 280 h holidays i hour/take-offs/landings j exercise/fun

23 Bullies at school

Exercise 2

1f 2e 3g 4c 5a 6j 7h 8b 9d 10i

Exercise 3

a2 b1 c3 d3

24 New foods

Exercise 2

1e 2g 3i 4h 5d 6f 7b 8a 9j 10c

Exercise 3

a3 b2 c3 d3 e1 f3

25 Too old to have children?

Exercise 2

a suffer b creating c doctors d someone who leaves school e not doing f expensive g probably h mean i damaged j stopped early

Exercise 3

a false b false c true d true e true f true g true h false i false j true

26 How deep can you go?

Exercise 2

1 apparatus 2 smashed 3 diver 4 rate 5 exhale 6 expand 7 depth 8 helium 9 magazines 10 squashes 11 submarines 12 sled 13 dioxide

Exercise 3

a true b false c false d false e true f false g true h true i false j false

27 Better school meals

Exercise 2

Across
7 appalling 8 lure 9 lasting 10 ditching

Down
1 pitta 2 junk 3 pair 4 piloted 5 salad 6 ban

Exercise 3

a1 b3 c3 d1

28 The 12-year-old alcoholic

Exercise 2

1e 2h 3i 4b 5g 6a 7c 8f 9d

Exercise 3

a alcopops/Stella Artois lager
b doors/walls/shout
c pass (black)/drunken (alcoholic)
d three/Survival
e trekking/cigarettes/drugs/friends
f two/own camp/food rations
g call centre/flat/school/Massachusetts (America)

29 Opportunities for wealth

Exercise 2

a stop it happening b a period of growth c dishonest d friendly e unhappy f you don't know what you are doing g profitable h a plantation i safe

Exercise 3

(a) 11,000,000,000 (eleven billion) (b) runway
(c) 140,000 (d) 0 (e) 0 (f) £200,000,000 (£200 million)
(g) cocoa (h) £3,000,000 (£3 million) (i) £50,000,000 (£50 million)

Exercise 5

1j 2g 3h 4a 5c 6i 7b 8e 9f 10d

Exercise 6

a science b knowledge c medicines d school e weapons f AIDS g man h debts i aid j look k actions

30 The old soldiers

Exercise 2

a get weaker b calm c your waist d sunset e interesting f enemies g sad h many i watching you j careful

Exercise 3

a false b false c false d true e true f false g true h false i true j true

31 Global warming

Exercise 2

a a soft sound b agree c weaker d keep going e very dangerous f empty g huge h the weather i extremely poor j empty

Exercise 3

a3 b1 c2 d1

32 Chemical alert

Exercise 2

1d 2a 3i 4h 5c 6g 7e 8j 9f 10b

Exercise 3

a1 b3 c2 d3

Material written by: Peter Dainty

Commissioning Editor: Jacquie Bloese

Editor: Matthew Hancock

Design and Illustration: www.mindseyedesign.co.uk

Cover Design: Eddie Rego

Photo Research: Mandi Kok, Emma Bree

Mary Glasgow Magazines (Scholastic Ltd.) grants teachers permission to photocopy the designated photocopiable pages from this book for classroom use. No other part of this publication may be reproduced in whole or in part, or stored in a retrieval system, or transmitted in any form or by any means, electronic, mechanical, photocopying, recording or otherwise, without written permission of the publisher. For information regarding permissions, write to:

Mary Glasgow Magazines (Scholastic Ltd.), Euston House, 24 Eversholt Street, London NW1 IDB.

© Scholastic Ltd. 2006   Reprinted in 2008.   All rights reserved.   Printed in the UK by Bell & Bain Ltd, Glasgow.

The publishers would like to thank the following for their kind permission to reprint articles and photographs:

Cover: © The Daily Telegraph, 2005, photographs; Empics.
BBC News
pp 70 - 71: © BBC News at bbcnews.co.uk. BBC News (online) 23/06/05
The Daily Express
pp 10 - 11: © Daily Express, 2004. 23/08/04
The Daily Mail
pp 18 - 19: © The Daily Mail/Solo Syndication. 12/08/03
pp 22 - 23: © The Daily Mail/Solo Syndication, photograph; © Caters News Agency. 08/11/04 pp 34 - 35: © The Daily Mail/Solo Syndication. The Daily Mail, Sunday Magazine. pp 38 - 39: © The Daily Mail/Solo Syndication. 31/10/03
pp 68 - 69: Mavrix photos. © The Daily Mail/Solo Syndication. 22/07/03
The Daily Mirror
pp 8 - 9: © mirrorpix. 5/01/89 pp 30 - 31: © mirrorpix. The People, 16/03/03
pp 62 - 63: © mirrorpix. 22/06/05 pp 76 - 77: © mirrorpix. 2/07/05
pp 82 - 83: © mirrorpix. 8/10/04
The Daily Telegraph
pp 32 - 33: ©The Daily Telegraph 2004, photographs; James Fraser. 28/04/04
pp 36 - 37: ©The Daily Telegraph 1998. 29/09/98 pp 48 - 51: Text and cartoon: © The Daily Telegraph 2004, photograph; David Burgess. 24/02/04 pp 52 - 53: © The Daily Telegraph 2003, photographs; John Lodge. 22/08/03 pp 56 - 57: © The Daily Telegraph 2005, photograph; James Fraser. 14/05/05 pp 74 - 75: © The Daily Telegraph 2004, with accompanying picture and graphic. 31/05/04
Evening Standard
pp 64 - 65: © Evening Standard. 31/05/05
Financial Times
pp 60 - 61: © Financial Times. 18/02/04
The Guardian
pp 20 - 21: © Guardian Newspapers Limited 1993. 13/04/93
pp 80 - 81: © Guardian Newspapers Limited 2005, photograph; Martin Godwin. 30/06/05

International Herald Tribune
pp 66 - 67: © International Herald Tribune.
The Independent
pp 14 - 15: © The Independent. 06/10/04
The Mail on Sunday
pp 12 - 13: © The Mail on Sunday/Solo Syndication. 13/02/05
The Sun
pp 24 - 25: Text and photograph: © NI Syndication 09/03/02
pp 28 - 29: © NI Syndication. 10/03/03 pp 42 - 43: Acknowledgement: Tessa Cunningham/Associated Newspapers. 1994 pp 44 - 45: Text and photograph: © NI Syndication. 21/02/03
pp 48 - 51: © NI Syndication. 24/02/04 pp 72 - 73: © NI syndication. 24/10/05
The Sunday Times
pp 54 - 55: © NI Syndication. 30/11/03
The Times
pp 16 - 17: © NI Syndication.1992 pp 16 - 17: © NI Syndication. 1992 pp 26 - 27: © Metropolitan Police. This article is no longer in use. pp 58 - 59: © NI Syndication. 25/10/04 pp 78 - 79: text and photograph: © NI Syndication. 05/06/04

Additional photos:
Cover photo: Digital Vision; Mary Glasgow Magazines; PA/Empics. **Page 4:** epa/Ansa. **Page 7:** K. Winter/Getty Images. **Page 8:** Stockbyte. **Page 11:** Hemera. **Page 12:** Hemera. **Page 14:** C. De Souza/AFP/Getty Images. **Page 16:** Image100. **Page 18:** Hemera. **Page 20:** Image100. **Page 26:** N. Munns/PA/Empics. **Page 28:** Photodisc. **Page 30:** Mary Glasgow Magazines. **Page 37:** P. Yates/Corbis. **Page 39:** K. Winter/Getty Images. **Page 43:** Rubberball. **Page 46:** Mary Glasgow Magazines. **Page 51:** D. Jones/PA/Empics. **Page 58:** epa/Ansa. **Page 61:** Hemera. **Page 63:** Image100. **Page 64:** Marks & Spencer; Hemera. **Page 67:** D. Pallages/AFP/Getty Images. **Page 70:** Getty Images. **Page 76:** J. Watson/Getty Images. **Page 83:** Mousetrap Media Ltd.

Every effort has been made to contact the copyright holders of the material used in this title. If any omissions have occurred, please contact the publishers who will be pleased to rectify the situation.